THE ABC GUIDE TO THE CORONATION

By the same Author:

Winston Churchill—a full-length biography
The Bernard Shaw Dictionary
The Way of the Dictators
Queens, Crowns and Coronations
The Innocence of Edith Thompson

John Somerville
from
Frances E. Daresbury

The ABC Guide to the Coronation

by

LEWIS BROAD

With Illustrations by

HAZEL COOK

Hutchinson
London

HUTCHINSON & CO. (PUBLISHERS) LTD.
London New York Toronto Melbourne
Sydney Cape Town

First published 1953

Printed in Great Britain by The Anchor Press, Ltd.,
Tiptree, Essex

HOW THE QUEEN IS CROWNED

I WANT first to describe the manner in which Queen Elizabeth will be crowned in Westminster Abbey on June 2. The ceremonial which will be followed is a very old one. It has been

Cover of the *Liber Regalis*

used for over a thousand years. The Kings of Saxon England were crowned and anointed very much in the same way. After the Conquest of England by the Normans the old rites were still used.

In the reign of Richard II (1377–1399) an account of the Coronation ceremonial was written down. This document is called the *Liber Regalis*, the Royal Book, which is one of the treasures kept by the Dean of Westminster. It gives a full description of the way in which the Sovereign was crowned nearly six hundred years ago, and ever since then the Coronations have followed that pattern.

The preparations in Westminster Abbey start long before the arrival of the Queen. The articles of the Regalia, the Crowns and the Sceptres and the Orbs and the other tokens of sovereign power are carried in procession to the West Door of the Abbey. Here the various Officers of State and Peers of the Realm who carry the Regalia assemble. On the arrival

The Recognition

of the Queen they all march from the West Door up the nave to the centre of the Abbey.

Here a platform, or theatre as it is called, has been erected. The Queen ascends the steps of the theatre and takes her seat upon the Chair of State. The Coronation ceremonial now begins with:

The Recognition. The Archbishop of Canterbury presents to the assembly in the Abbey the Queen as rightful inheritor of the Crown of the Realm, and he asks whether those present are willing to do their homage and bounden duty. This inquiry is made four times, one at each side of the theatre. The Queen turns herself so that she may face that section of the congregation which the Primate is addressing. At the end of each invitation the congregation, led by the Queen's Scholars of Westminster School, raise a great shout. At former coronations the Litany was said and a sermon preached by one of the bishops, but changes have been made in recent times, as a result of which, following the Recognition,

The Oath

The Oath is administered to Her Majesty, who promises to govern the people according to their laws and customs, and to maintain the laws of God and the Protestant Reformed religion. The Queen goes from the theatre to the Altar, and laying her right hand upon the Holy Gospel, takes the Oath, kisses the Bible, and signs the Oath.

The Anointing follows. The Queen, having been disrobed of her crimson robe, seats herself in King Edward's Chair, or the Coronation Chair, which stands in front of the Altar. Four Knights of the Garter hold over her a rich pall of silk or cloth-of-gold. The Dean of Westminster takes the Ampulla and Spoon from the altar and pours some of the Holy Oil from the Ampulla into the Spoon. The Archbishop dips his fingers into the Oil in the Spoon and anoints the Queen on the crown of the head and on the palms of both hands. The Queen is then attired in the Colobium Sindonis and in the Supertunica.

Spurs and Sword are presented. The Spurs are presented by the Lord Great Chamberlain and the Queen forthwith

The Anointing

sends them back to the altar. The Sword is delivered into her right hand by the Archbishop of Canterbury. After a prayer the Queen, going to the altar, offers the Sword there in the scabbard and then returns to her seat in King Edward's Chair. The Sword is redeemed for 100 shillings by the peer who bore it in the procession and, receiving it from the Dean of Westminster, the peer draws it out of the scabbard and carries it naked before the Queen during the rest of the solemnity. Next is

The Investing of the Sovereign. First the Armill and Robe Royal, or Pall of Cloth-of-Gold, are put upon the Queen by the Dean of Westminster, the Lord Great Chamberlain

The Queen receiving the Sword

fastening the clasps. The Ring, known as the Wedding Ring of England, is put upon the fourth finger of the Queen's right hand. The Archbishop delivers the Sceptre with the Cross into the Queen's right hand, and the Sceptre with Dove into her left hand. Then follows

Putting on the Crown. The Archbishop takes the Crown from the Dean, and reverently places it upon the Queen's head. At this the congregation raise repeated shouts of "God Save the Queen!" The Peers, Peeresses, and the Kings of Arms put on their coronets. The trumpets sound and the guns at the Tower of London fire a Royal Salute. The Holy Bible is presented to the Queen by the Archbishop, and the Queen, having thus been anointed and crowned, and having received all the ensigns of Royalty, is solemnly blessed.

The Enthronization is the next ceremony. The Queen returns from the Altar to the theatre and is lifted up into her Throne by the Archbishops, the Bishops, and Peers of the Kingdom.

Fealty is now rendered by the Archbishop of Canterbury on behalf of the Lords Spiritual—that is the Bishops and the

Investing the Sovereign

officiating prelates—and the Archbishop kisses the Queen's left cheek. The Peers then do their **Homage**, the first Peer of each Order doing homage on behalf of his fellows—first the Princes of the Blood Royal, then the Dukes, followed by the Marquesses, Earls, Viscounts, and finally the Barons. When the Homage is ended, the drums beat, the trumpets sound, and the people shout "God Save the Queen!"

The Communion Service is resumed. The Queen returns to the steps at the altar, and takes off her crown. She makes an oblation or offering of a pall or altar cloth and an ingot or wedge of gold of a pound weight.

The Communion Service ended, the Queen, with the four Swords borne before her, and carrying her Sceptre and Rod, goes into St. Edward's Chapel. There the articles of the Regalia are placed upon the altar. The Queen is disrobed of her Royal Robe of State, and is arrayed in her robe of purple velvet.

Then, wearing her Imperial Crown, and bearing in her left

hand the Orb and in her right hand the Sceptre with Cross, she marches to the West Door of the Abbey. At the entrance to the Abbey Her Majesty takes her place in her coach for the return drive to Buckingham Palace.

Details of the various Coronation ceremonies, and explanations of the ancient names, will be found in the dictionary following.

Rendering of Homage by Peers of the Realm

ABC GUIDE TO THE CEREMONIES

A

ACCESSION. The Sovereign's accession to the English Throne follows immediately upon the death of the previous monarch. The ceremony which marks the beginning of a new reign is the holding of the Accession Council. King George V died at Sandringham on January 20, 1936; on the following day the Prince of Wales, as the new King, Edward VIII, flew from Sandringham and attended the Accession Council at St. James's Palace. The Council consisted of Lords Spiritual and Temporal, members of the Privy Council, the Lord Mayor and Aldermen of London, and "Numbers of other principal Gentlemen of Quality", reinforced by representatives of the Dominions, whose presence testified to the new relations with the Motherland established under the Statute of Westminster. The Council "with one Voice and Consent of Tongue and Heart" proclaimed the high and mighty Prince Edward Albert Christian George Andrew Patrick David to be "our only lawful and rightful Liege Lord Edward the Eighth".

Thereafter King Edward made a brief declaration to the Privy Council, pledging himself to strive to follow in the footsteps of his father. He said:

> "Through the irreparable loss which the British Commonwealth of Nations has sustained by the death of His Majesty, my beloved father, has devolved upon me the duty of sovereignty. I know how much you and all my subjects, with, I hope I may say, the whole world, feel for me in my sorrow, and I am confident in the affectionate sympathy which will be extended to my dear mother in her overpowering grief.
>
> "When my father stood here twenty-six years ago he declared that one of the objects of his life would be to uphold constitutional government. In this I am determined to follow in my father's footsteps and to work as he did throughout his life for the happiness and welfare of all classes of my subjects.
>
> "I place my reliance upon the loyalty and affection of my peoples throughout the Empire, and upon the wisdom of their Parliaments,

to support me in this heavy task, and I pray that God will guide me to perform it."

The King then took the oath providing for the security of the Church of Scotland. The accession was complete.

In the case of King George VI, the Accession Council was held on Saturday, December 12, 1936, the abdication of King Edward VIII having taken effect on the preceding day. King George made the following declaration to the Council:

"I meet you today in circumstances which are without parallel in the history of our country. Now that the duties of sovereignty have fallen to me, I declare to you my adherence to the strict principles of constitutional government and my resolve to work before all else for the welfare of the British Commonwealth of Nations.

"With my wife as helpmeet by my side, I take up the heavy task which lies before me. In it I look for the support of all my peoples. Furthermore, my first act on succeeding my brother will be to confer on him a Dukedom, and he will henceforth be known as His Royal Highness the Duke of Windsor."

George VI died in his sleep in the early hours of February 6, 1952. Princess Elizabeth, without knowing it, had become Queen at the age of twenty-five, while spending the night observing jungle animals from the Treetops Hotel, a four-room bungalow built in a giant fig tree in the Aberdare Forest game reserve in Kenya. This accession, unique in history, was the first to take place abroad for more than two hundred years—since the Elector of Hanover was summoned to England in 1714 to become George I.

It had been 115 years since a Sovereign Queen had ascended the Throne and 51 years since the country had a Queen as ruler. The five previous Sovereign Queens, or Queens Regnant, were:

Mary I .	. 1553–1558
Elizabeth I	. 1558–1603
Mary II	. 1689–1694
Anne .	. 1702–1714
Victoria	. 1837–1901

Queen Elizabeth II acceded while she was with the Duke of Edinburgh in Kenya on the first stage of their projected tour of Australia and New Zealand, which they were to have made in place of King George VI because of His Majesty's state of health. As soon as she heard of her father's death, the young Queen flew home. She was delayed by thunderstorms but arrived in London on February 7. Next day she was publicly proclaimed Queen.

The form of the Queen's title used in the Proclamation attracted attention. It was:

> "Queen of this Realm and of her other Realms and Territories, Head of the Commonwealth, Defender of the Faith."

It was the first time the phrase "Head of the Commonwealth" had been used in proclaiming the Sovereign. A few days later, in appointing her first Royal Commission to convey Royal assent to Parliamentary Bills, the Queen used the following traditional title in her proclamation to the House of Lords:

> "Elizabeth Regina, Elizabeth the Second, by the Grace of God, of Great Britain, Ireland and of the British Dominions Beyond the Seas Queen, Defender of the Faith."

The title Empress of India, first assumed by Queen Victoria in 1877, no longer followed Defender of the Faith.

In her Accession Declaration before the Accession Council in St. James's Palace on February 8, 1952, the Queen said:

> "By the sudden death of my dear father, I am called to assume the duties and responsibilities of sovereignty. At this time of deep sorrow, it is a profound consolation to me to be assured of the sympathy which you and all my peoples feel towards me, to my mother, and my sister, and to the other members of my family.
>
> "My father was our revered and beloved head, as he was of the wider family of his subjects: the grief which his loss brings is shared among us all. My heart is too full for me to say more to you today than that I shall always work, as my father did throughout his reign, to uphold constitutional government and to advance the happiness and prosperity of my peoples, spread as they are all the world over.
>
> "I know that in my resolve to follow his shining example of

service and devotion I shall be inspired by the loyalty and affection of those whose Queen I have been called to be and by the counsel of their elected Parliaments.

"I pray that God will help me to discharge worthily this heavy task that has been laid upon me so early in life."

ALFRED'S CROWN. Traditionally supposed to have been the ancient Crown of England which was destroyed at the time of the Commonwealth. According to the historians the Crown was conferred on Alfred when he visited Rome as a child of five in the year 853 and was crowned by Pope Leo. The crown of the King of Wessex is supposed to have been inherited by the line of Saxon Kings, to have been used by Edward the Confessor, and to have survived until its destruction with the other Crown Jewels in the time of Oliver Cromwell, when the articles of gold were melted down and sold for what the precious metal would fetch. In the inventory which was drawn up occurs the entry: "King Alfred's Crown of goulde wyerworke set with slight stones and 2 little bells—£248 10*s.* 0*d.*"

Alfred's Crown

AMICE. Square piece of linen placed upon the Sovereign's head immediately after the ceremony of the anointing with oil. It is also called the coif. According to the ancient ritual it had to remain on the Sovereign's head for seven days. On the eighth day it was removed and then "the Bishop shall wash the King's head carefully with hot water and after washing it and drying it he shall reverently arrange the King's hair. Then shall be put the golden circlet on the King's head with all honour: and the circlet shall be worn all that day in reverence of his cleansing." The word "amice" is derived from the Latin word that means mantle or cloak. A vestment worn by the priest at Mass is called amice.

AMPULLA. Receptacle of gold in the form of an eagle which contains the oil for the anointing of the Sovereign. The eagle, with outspread wings, stands on a pedestal, the total height being nine inches and the weight ten ounces. The head

Ampulla

unscrews to permit the insertion of the oil. It will contain about six ounces. The oil is poured out of the beak into a spoon into which the Archbishop dips his fingers, and then anoints the Queen on head and hands. The word "ampulla" is a Latin one, being the name of the globular vessel the Romans used for holding liquids and ointments. It is applied to the cruet used for water and wine at Mass. The Ampulla and Spoon are older than the other objects of the Regalia, being relics of the articles in use before the Commonwealth, during which the Regalia was destroyed.

ANNE, PRINCESS, second child of Queen Elizabeth and the Duke of Edinburgh, born Clarence House, August 15, 1950. (*See under* ROYAL FAMILY.)

ANOINTING. Anointing the Sovereign with consecrated oil is a very ancient feature of the Coronation ceremonial. It was carried out among the Egyptians over 6000 years ago. Among the Christian peoples of the Western world, anointing is first known to have been used at coronations in Spain some 1200 years ago. A hundred years later it was employed in certain of the kingdoms of England. The rite was certainly carried out for Alfred the Great by the Pope, Leo IV, for the old chronicler records that the Pope "oiled him to be King".

According to the earliest English rite the King was simply anointed on the head. Later there was a five-fold anointing of the hands, the breast, the shoulder, the elbows, and last of all the head. Richard the Lion Heart was stripped to his shirt to receive the holy unction. The boy King Edward VI was laid upon the altar of the Abbey for Archbishop Cranmer to anoint his back.

For the carrying out of the anointing ceremony the Sovereign is disrobed while Handel's anthem "Zadok the Priest" is sung. The Lord Great Chamberlain removes the crimson robe, which he delivers to the Master of the Robes. The Queen herself takes off her Cap of State, which is given by the Lord Great Chamberlain to the Chamberlain of the Household. Robe and Cap are carried into St. Edward's Chapel by the Groom of the Robes.

Then the Queen sits before the altar in King Edward's Chair covered with cloth-of-gold. At the summons of Garter King-of-Arms, four Knights of the Garter approach to hold over her head the rich canopy of cloth-of-gold. Now the Dean of Westminster takes from the altar the Ampulla and pours out some oil into the Anointing Spoon with which the Archbishop anoints the Queen in the form of a cross

On the palms of both the hands, saying:

"Be thy Hands anointed with holy oil."

On the crown of the head saying:

"Be thy Head anointed with holy oil, as kings, priests, and prophets were anointed.

Knights of the Garter holding the Canopy over the Queen

"And as Solomon was anointed King by Zadok the priest and Nathan the prophet, so be you anointed, blessed, and consecrated Queen over the Peoples, whom the Lord your God hath given you to rule and govern. In the Name of the Father, and of the Son, and of the Holy Ghost. Amen."

Then, the Queen kneeling, the Primate pronounces a blessing over her, asking that the works of her hands may be prospered "and that by the assistance of His heavenly grace you may preserve the people committed to your charge in wealth, peace, and godliness".

The holy oil, or chrism, was regarded in ancient times with much veneration. Great care was taken in its preparation from oil mingled with balm consecrated by a bishop. So much sanctity was attached to the ceremonial that the piece of linen with which any excess of oil was wiped away after the anointing had to be burned, lest the oil be polluted. At one time a cap was placed over the anointed head and had to remain for a space of seven days.

When Henry VII was crowned it was provided that after the anointing his head should be "washed, dryed, and cymbed" with the ivory comb of St. Edward "if the King's hair lie not smooth". At the coronation of Queen Elizabeth I it was complained that the holy oil was not of proper quality—it was "greese and smelt ill". There was no such complaint over the unction compounded for King James II, who was so pleased with the fragrance of the preparation of his apothecary that he rewarded him with a fee of £200. In modern coronations a plain olive oil is employed.

AQUAMARINE MONDE, Or ORB, was a superb jewel which was said to surmount the crown up to about a century ago. Investigations at that time showed that the superb jewel was nothing but glass. This gem is still shown amongst the Crown Jewels in the Tower. What has become of the original stone is a mystery. One suggestion to account for its disappearance is that when James II escaped from England to France he took with him the Aquamarine Monde and replaced it with a piece of blue glass.

ARMILL. There are two articles in the Coronation ceremonial to which this name is applied. The word in the Coronation ceremony is a matter of some mystery. It is a Latin one meaning bracelet, but though there are a fine pair of bracelets in the Regalia, they are not now used, the last Coronation at which they were employed being that of Edward VI, in 1547. The term is also applied to the Stole, a narrow strip of silk, something like a scarf, which is passed over the Sovereign's shoulders and the back of the neck. How the Stole came to be called the Armill is a Coronation curiosity.

B

BALMORAL CASTLE. The private property of the Sovereign, Balmoral Castle, on Deeside in West Aberdeenshire, was Queen Victoria's favourite residence. Prince Albert bought the 11,000-acre estate in 1852 for £31,500 and the Castle was rebuilt three years later. Queen Victoria often held Court there and since then the Royal Family have kept up the

Balmoral Castle

annual custom of staying at Balmoral in the shooting season. The sporting estate abounds with grouse and red deer.

BARONS OF THE CINQUE PORTS. In latter years the Barons of the Cinque Ports have had to reconsider their Coronation claim. Their ancient request was to carry over the Sovereign in the coronation procession a canopy of cloth-of-gold or purple silk, ornamented with silver-gilt bells and borne upon four staves; according to a Twelfth-century record this was the Cinque Ports' reward for the services they had rendered to King John on his voyages to and from Normandy. But with the abandonment of the Westminster Hall ceremonial the Barons have had to claim—"if Canopies are not used"—to be assigned a station within the Abbey and to attend on the Sovereign. Looking back on history, we find the Barons putting up a vigorous fight for their rights on various occasions. They had to scrimmage with the royal footmen at Charles II's Coronation in order to retain the canopy; at the crowning of William and Mary and of George III, however, they lost their privileged places near the Sovereign at the banquet. The Cinque Ports today embrace Dover, Hastings, Hythe, Romney, Sandwich, Rye, and Winchelsea. (*See also* CINQUE PORTS, LORD WARDEN OF THE.)

BATH AND WELLS, BISHOP OF. Shares with the Bishop of Durham the privilege of attending the Sovereign during the procession to Westminster Abbey and the Coronation ceremony. This right has been exercised at successive Coronations since the time of Richard I with only two recorded exceptions, those of Henry VII and William III. The present Bishop is the Rt. Rev. Harold William Bradfield, the seventy-second occupant of the see, appointed in 1946 at the age of forty-eight, the youngest Bishop in the Church. For over ten years he was Secretary of the Canterbury Diocesan Board of Finance, 1934–44. He was born on September 20, 1898, married in 1922 and has two sons and two daughters. He was Archdeacon of Croydon from 1942 to 1946.

BEDCHAMBER, LADIES AND WOMEN OF. The former are Peeresses whose only duties now are attendance at courts and ceremonials. Women of the Bedchamber are also of high rank and one is always in residential personal attendance on Her Majesty. Up to the time of George II the Women of the Bedchamber were present at the Queen's toilet. Now both the Ladies and the Women of the Bedchamber are styled Ladies in Waiting.

BIBLE—Is presented to the Sovereign following the placing of the Crown upon the head. This ceremony was first introduced at the Coronation of William and Mary. As the Archbishop presents the copy of the Holy Scriptures he says: "Our Gracious Queen, we present you with this Book, the most valuable thing that this world affords. Here is Wisdom; This is the Royal Law; These are the lively Oracles of God."

BLACK PRINCE'S RUBY. One of the most famous stones in the English Regalia, now displayed in the Imperial State Crown above the Second Star of Africa. Six hundred years ago this ruby was one of the treasures which cost the King of Granada his life, for he was murdered by Pedro the Cruel of Castille, who coveted his jewels. It was presented by Don Pedro to the Black Prince, son of King Edward III, in the year 1367 in recognition of the help given by the English knights at the Battle of Najara. It was then added to the Regalia and was worn in his helmet by King Henry V at the Battle of Agincourt. Somehow it survived the chances of the Commonwealth and found its place in Charles II's Regalia. It narrowly escaped loss when Colonel Blood made his raid on the Crown Jewels, but was discovered in the pocket of one of Blood's associates.

Black Rod

BLACK ROD, GENTLEMAN USHER OF THE. Chief Usher of the Court and the Kingdom, and an important official of the House of Lords. The title is derived from the staff of office, an ebony rod surmounted with a golden lion. The first Black Rod was appointed in 1350. This official is the senior of the Gentlemen Ushers Daily Waiters, who wait next to the person of the monarch in the Presence Chamber; they rank after the Lord Chamberlain and the Vice-Chamberlain. On account of his parliamentary duties, Black Rod is excused attendance on the Sovereign. In the House of Lords Black Rod is present to maintain order. When the House of Commons is summoned to the House of Lords for the Royal Assent to Bills, or when the Queen's Speech is being delivered from the Throne or read in the Sovereign's absence, Black Rod acts as messenger to the Commons from the Lords. This formality—one of great historic interest—proceeds as follows: When Black Rod approaches, the doors of the Commons are closed against him. Thereupon he knocks thrice and announces himself. Admitted, he acquaints the House with the purpose of his visit. This ceremony, which originated after Charles I had attempted to arrest five members of the Commons in

Bracelets

1642, signifies the freedom of the Lower House from interference from the Upper House. At the Coronation procession within the Abbey, Black Rod walks before the Lord Great Chamberlain and after the bearers of the Regalia. The present Gentleman Usher of the Black Rod is Lieut.-Gen. Sir Brian Horrocks, K.C.B., K.B.E., D.S.O., M.C., who was appointed in 1949. He was born in 1896. In the Second World War as a tank expert he commanded a corps in the pursuit from El Alamein and later in Normandy, and in the dramatic armoured drives through Belgium, Holland, and into Germany. He was G.O.C.-in-C. British Army of the Rhine in 1948, but ill-health caused by grave wounds in an air raid at Bizerta, Tunisia, compelled him to retire after seventeen days in the post. The Yeoman Usher is Black Rod's deputy.

BRACELETS. There are a fine pair in the Regalia, but they are not now used at the Coronation ceremony. The last

Buckingham Palace

occasion on which they were used was at the crowning of the boy King Edward VI in 1547. Nevertheless, after the Restoration a new pair was made to replace those destroyed in the Commonwealth. They are of solid gold, lined with crimson velvet, richly enamelled and bearing the emblems of England, Scotland, Ireland, and the fleur-de-lis of France. From very ancient times bracelets have been regarded as symbols of sovereignty.

BUCKINGHAM PALACE. Buckingham House, as it was then called, was bought by George III for £21,000 in 1761 from John Sheffield, Duke of Buckingham. The mansion was altered from time to time, and it was not until Queen Victoria's day that it was used continually as the royal residence. The East Wing was added in 1846. The present façade was designed by Sir Aston Webb in 1912 and cost £60,000. During the Second World War fourteen bombing incidents occurred at the Palace.

BUTLER, THE CHIEF. Since the abandonment of the Coronation banquet in Westminster Hall, the office of Chief Butler of England has fallen into disuse. It was formerly an office of considerable importance, for the Chief Butler had to protect the King from being poisoned. At the Coronation of

King Edward VII the petitions of three claimants—the Duke of Norfolk as Earl of Arundel, Baron Mowbray, Segrave, and Stourton, and Mr. F. O. Taylor, lord of the manor of Kenninghall, Norfolk—were recorded but not adjudicated upon, since the Chief Butler's duties no longer existed.

C

CANOPY. It was formerly the custom for a Canopy to be borne over the Sovereign as he marched in procession from Westminster Hall to the Abbey for his Coronation. Originally it was a square of purple silk carried on four silver lances, the bearers being the Barons of the Cinque Ports, four of whom were assigned to each lance. Since the Coronation of George IV in 1821 the procession from Westminster Hall to the Abbey has been dispensed with, and there has been no occasion for the canopy to be borne. A rich Pall of silk or cloth-of-gold, a kind of small Canopy, is held over the Sovereign by four Knights of the Garter as she sits in the Coronation Chair to be anointed.

CANTERBURY, ARCHBISHOP OF. By right of his office conducts the Coronation Service, places the Crown upon the head of the Sovereign, and anoints her with oil. The Archbishop of Canterbury is the principal officer of the English Church, being Primate of All England, whereas the Archbishop of York is Primate of England. The former is styled Archbishop by Divine Providence, while the Archbishop of York is addressed by Divine Permission. The See was founded by St. Augustine in the year 597, and the present Archbishop, the Most Rev. and Rt. Hon. Geoffrey Francis Fisher, P.C., D.D., is the ninety-ninth of the line. He was appointed in 1945 on the death of Dr. Temple. Dr. Fisher officiated at the wedding of the Queen, as Princess Elizabeth, and the Duke of Edinburgh in 1947. Prince Charles was baptized by him at Buckingham Palace in the following year. In February 1952 the Archbishop rose from a sick-bed to

Archbishop of Canterbury

conduct the funeral service for King George VI at St. George's Chapel, Windsor. Dr. Fisher, who was born in 1887, achieved the distinction of becoming Archbishop of Canterbury in little over twelve years after consecration as a bishop and without having held a benefice. He was Headmaster of Repton from 1914 to 1932, Bishop of Chester 1932–9, and then Bishop of London until his appointment as Archbishop. Son of a rector, he was educated at Marlborough and Exeter College, Oxford. From 1939 to 1945 he was Dean of the Chapels Royal. He was married in 1917 and has six sons. His Grace signs himself Geoffrey Cantuar, his Christian name and the name of his arch-diocese in Latin. During a long succession of coronations the Archbishop of Canterbury has received as fee the purple velvet chair, cushion and footstool which he uses at the ceremony.

Coronation Chair

CAP OF MAINTENANCE. An emblem of royal dignity which is carried before the Sovereign on various occasions of State. It is made of crimson velvet, and is trimmed with ermine. The Marquess of Winchester, premier marquess of England, has the hereditary privilege of bearing this emblem. At former coronations the Sovereign wore the Cap of Maintenance while the sermon was preached. The lining of the crowns and of the coronets of peers resembles the Cap of Maintenance.

CHAIR OF CORONATION, or King Edward's Chair, is occupied by the Queen during her anointing and crowning. It is placed for her reception immediately before the altar in the Abbey. It was made during the reign of Edward I to receive the Stone of Scone (*q.v.*), which that King captured from the Scots. It is kept in the Abbey near the foot of the shrine of Edward the Confessor, and has only twice been

Chair of State

taken out of the Abbey—for use by Oliver Cromwell when he was inaugurated as Lord Protector in Westminster Hall in 1657, and during the Second World War, when it was removed for safety to Gloucester Cathedral. The Chair was made about the year 1297 by Adam, the King's workman, from English oak at a cost of 100 shillings.

At each coronation it is covered with cloth-of-gold, and it bears the holes made by nails used during the centuries to affix the cloth. The Sovereign occupies the Chair only during the anointing, investing, and crowning ceremonies; thereafter she sits on the throne provided for her on the raised platform or theatre. The Coronation Chair was first used for the crowning of Edward II in 1307. It has been occupied by every Sovereign since with the exception of the boy King Edward V, who was murdered in the Tower and never crowned, and

Chalice

Edward VIII, who abdicated before the date fixed for his Coronation; with the possible exception also of Henry Tudor, and the certain exception of Mary, wife of William of Orange, for whom a special chair was constructed.

CHAIR OF STATE. This is provided for the Sovereign on the theatre. She sits in it until she has received her crown; thereafter she takes her seat on the throne.

CHALICE. Used during the service of Communion following the Coronation. The Chalice is the vessel which contains the consecrated wine, and the Paten is the shallow dish holding the bread or wafer. During the procession from the West Door of the Abbey, Chalice and Paten are carried in front of the Queen by two bishops. The Chalice is a gold vessel eighteen inches in height, with a handle and cover. It is embossed with the faces of cherubs, foliage, and festoons of fruit and roses. On the front is the cipher of William and Mary, surmounted by a royal crown, both the Chalice and the Paten having been made for William and Mary in 1692. They are placed on the altar of St. Peter ad Vincula in the Tower on the three great festivals of the Church — Easter Day, Whit Sunday, and Christmas Day. The altar-plate thus displaced dates from the time of Charles I and Charles II. The reason for the custom is unknown.

Child of the Chapel Royal

Champion. (*See* King's Champion.)

CHARLES, PRINCE, son and heir of Queen Elizabeth and the Duke of Edinburgh, born Buckingham Palace November 14, 1948. (*See under* Royal Family.)

CHESTER, EARL OF. One of the titles traditional to the eldest son of the Sovereign, It is conferred at the same time as the Sovereign creates the Heir Apparent Prince of Wales.

CHILDREN OF THE CHAPEL. Name given to the choirboys of the Chapels Royal.

CINQUE PORTS, LORD WARDEN OF THE. Dover, Sandwich, Hastings, Romney, and Hythe were originally the cinque (five) ports; Winchelsea, Rye, and other places were later added to the group. After the Norman Conquest, William I put this part of the south-east coast of England in the keeping of a warden, whose word was law in the area, and who had to provide ships for the King when called upon. The wide powers of the Lord Warden of the Cinque Ports have long since been curtailed, but he still has maritime jurisdiction as Admiral of the Cinque Ports, and can appoint Justices of the Peace for the area. The Lord Warden is installed in office by the "Grand Court of Shepway", a survival of the Courts formerly held at Shepway Cross, near Lympne.

This ancient court sat at Dover in 1946 to install Mr. Winston Churchill, the present Lord Warden. King George VI appointed him in 1941 to succeed the late Marquess of Willingdon. The appointment is the Sovereign's personal prerogative, and it was understood to be His Majesty's own wish that, as a mark of appreciation for his services to the nation, Mr. Churchill should fill the oldest office associated with the defence of the realm. Mr. Churchill attended the funeral of George VI in the uniform of the Lord Warden. The post carries no salary but the holder can occupy the official residence at Walmer Castle.

CIVIL LIST. This is the annual income granted to the Sovereign to meet personal expenses and maintain the Royal Household. George III surrendered hereditary revenues with certain exceptions, retaining particularly those of the Duchies of Cornwall and Lancaster, and in return received a fixed Civil List of £800,000. Out of this the Sovereign in those days had to meet many additional large expenses, such as salaries and costs of embassies abroad and of Judges, which have since been borne by the Exchequer. The royal income is fixed by Parliament early in each reign. The Queen's Civil List, voted by Parliament six months after the reign began,

Clarence House

amounts to £475,000, compared with £410,000 received by George VI. It is made up as follows:

Her Majesty's Privy Purse	£60,000
Salaries of Her Majesty's Household	£185,000
Expenses of Her Majesty's Household	£121,800
Royal Bounty	£13,200
Supplementary Provision	£95,000

By separate provision the Duke of Edinburgh receives £40,000 a year. Parliament also decided that the net revenues of the Duchy of Cornwall should be applied during the minority of the Duke of Cornwall in relief of the Civil List, subject to a prior annual charge of one-ninth for the Duke's maintenance and education and accumulation of a moderate capital sum on his majority. This charge represents £150,000 until the Duke's eighteenth birthday. In the last three years of his minority he will receive a further £30,000 a year.

CLARENCE HOUSE. Adjoining St. James's Palace, Clarence House was reconstructed for the Duke of Clarence, later William IV, in 1825 from the old portion of the palace in Stable Yard. Previously the Duke, third son of George III, lived in apartments on the site. He became King at Clarence House in 1830 and reigned till his death in 1837 at the age of seventy-one. Later Queen Victoria's mother, the Duchess of Kent, lived there. From 1866 to 1893 it was the home of Queen Victoria's second son, the Duke of Edinburgh. In 1900 it passed to the first Duke of Connaught till his death in 1942. Then for five years the house was the headquarters of the Red Cross and St. John organization. When it was chosen as Princess Elizabeth's home after her marriage, Parliament granted £50,000 for its modernization. On July 4, 1949, more than eighteen months after their marriage, the Queen, then Princess Elizabeth, and the Duke of Edinburgh took up residence there until Easter 1952. Princess Anne, on August 15, 1950, was the first baby to be born in Clarence House since its conversion by Nash 125 years earlier. A daughter of the Duke of Clarence, Princess Elizabeth, was born in 1820 in the older building. She died a few months later. Had she survived she would have reigned as Elizabeth II; instead her cousin, Victoria, ascended the Throne.

CLERK OF THE CROWN. This is an office of immemorial antiquity. From the earliest times the Clerk of the Crown has recorded the judgments of the Court of Claims and been present at the Coronation to compile the official record known as the Coronation Roll. The present Clerk of the Crown is Sir Albert Napier, K.C.B., Q.C. The Clerk's petition to the Court of Claims runs as follows: "To record the proceedings in Westminster Abbey and to be assigned a suitable place therein to discharge his duties, and that the Registrar of the Privy Council may be associated with, and assistant to, the Clerk for this purpose. Also to have five yards of scarlet cloth."

COACH OF STATE, or CORONATION COACH. Queen Elizabeth will drive to and from Westminster Abbey for her Coronation in the Coach of State, which is nearly two hundred years old. It was built for King George III and was designed by Sir William Chambers, R.A., who recommended Joseph Wilton, R.A., and Mr. Pugello to conduct the building of the carriage on premises in Queen Anne Street, East. The model was executed from Chambers's design by Laurence Anderson Holme, a Dane. The carriage is composed of four tritons, which support the body by cables; the two placed on

Coach of State

the front bear the driver on their shoulders, and are sounding-shells; and those on the back part carry the imperial fasces, topped with tridents. The driver's footboard is a large scallop-shell, supported by marine plants. The pole resembles a bundle of lances; and the wheels are in imitation of those of ancient triumphal chariots. The body of the coach is composed of eight palm trees, which, branching out at the top, sustain the roof: at each angle are trophies of British victories. On the centre of the roof stand boy genii of England, Scotland, and Ireland, supporting the Imperial Crown, and holding the Sceptre, the Sword of State, and ensigns of knighthood; f their bodies festoons of laurel fall thence to the four corners of the roof. The intervals between the palm trees, which form the body of the coach, are filled in the upper part with plate-glass, and the panels below with paintings as follows:

Front Panel—Britannia on a throne holding a staff of liberty, attended by Religion, Justice, Wisdom, Valour, Fortitude, Commerce, Plenty, and Victory, presenting her with a garland of laurel. Background, St. Paul's and the Thames.

The left door of the Coach of State

Right Door—Industry and Ingenuity giving a cornucopia to the Genius of England. Side Panels—History recording the reports of Fame, and Peace burning the implements of War. Back Panel—Neptune and Amphitrite in a car drawn by sea-horses, attended by the Winds, Rivers, Tritons, Naiads, etc., bringing the tribute of the world to Britain. Upper Part of Back Panel—The Royal Arms, ornamented with the Order of St. George, the Golden Fleece, the rose, shamrock, and thistle entwined.

Left Door—Mars, Minerva, and Mercury supporting the imperial crown. Side Panels—The Arts and Sciences.

The body is lined with scarlet embossed velvet, superbly

laced and embroidered with the Star, encircled by the collar, of the Order of the Garter, and surmounted by the Imperial Crown, pendent the George and Dragon; in the corners, the rose, shamrock, and thistle entwined. The badges of St. Michael, St. George, the Guelph and Bath, St. Andrew, and St. Patrick are also among the embroidery. The hammer cloth is of scarlet velvet, with gold badges, ropes, and tassels. The length of the carriage and body is 24 feet; width, 8 feet 3 inches; height, 12 feet; length of pole, 12 feet 4 inches; weight, 4 tons. The carving was mostly executed by Nicholas Collett, a man of small stature, whom Waldron the actor (originally a carver in wood) delighted to call "a Garrick of a carver". The panels were painted by Cipriani, who received £800. The whole cost was as follows:

	£	*s.*	*d.*
Coachmaker, including Wheelwright and Smith	1637	15	0
Carver	2500	0	0
Gilder	935	14	0
Painter	315	0	0
Laceman	737	10	7
Chaser	665	4	6
Harness-maker	375	15	0
Mercer	202	5	10½
Beltmaker	99	6	6
Milliner	31	3	4
Saddler	10	16	6
Woollendraper	4	3	6
Covermaker	3	9	6
	£7518	4	3½

The bill was £8000, but, being taxed, was reduced as above, the odd pence arising from the ribbon weaver's bill.

COLLEGE OF ARMS, or HERALDS' COLLEGE, is a department of the Royal Household under the jurisdiction of the Earl Marshal, the Duke of Norfolk. It is the sole authority on behalf of the Sovereign on all matters of heraldry, the bearing of arms, and precedence. Its officials proclaim the accession of the Sovereign and assist the Earl Marshal in making the arrangements for the Coronation, and for State

Garter King of Arms

ceremonies such as royal marriages, funerals, openings of Parliament. In 1934 the corporate body of the College of Arms, whose headquarters are in Queen Victoria Street, E.C.4, celebrated the 450th anniversary of the granting of its charter by King Richard III, which made the College the sole arbiter in matters of arms and precedence. Its members, who hold office by Letters Patent under the Great Seal of England, practise heraldic matters on their own account for fees. The officials of the College of Arms, acting through the Earl Marshal, consist of three Kings of Arms, six Heralds, and four Pursuivants.

The Kings of Arms are the chief officials of the College, and of these the principal is *Garter King of Arms*, at present Sir George Rothe Bellew, C.V.O. This office was created by Henry V in 1417. It takes its name from the Order of the Garter, of which the holder is principal officer of arms. The two other Kings of Arms share the heraldic jurisdiction of the country between them. South of the River Trent is the province of Clarenceux King of Arms, an office first created as Clarenceux Herald by King Edward III. The name is derived from the dukedom of his son, the Duke of Clarence. When Edward IV succeeded to the dukedom on the death of his brother he made the herald *Clarenceux King of Arms*. The present holder is Sir Arthur William Steuart Cochrane, K.C.V.O.

North of the Trent is the territory of *Norroy King of Arms*, whose title comes from a corruption of two French words meaning north king. The office first came into use in the time of King Edward III, and was made permanent by King Edward IV. The present Norroy and Ulster King of Arms is Sir Gerald Wollaston, K.C.B., K.C.V.O.

The office of herald is of great antiquity. Originally the herald was a messenger between armies; today he is the maker of proclamations. Heralds do not, as is popularly supposed, play trumpets. This duty preliminary to the herald's function is discharged by trumpeters. The six heralds of the College of Heralds are:

Chester, an office founded in the reign of Edward III, now held by Mr. John Dunamace Heaton-Armstrong, M.V.O.

Windsor, also founded by Edward III, held by Mr. Richard Preston Graham-Vivian, M.C.

Somerset, founded in 1502 by King Henry VII in honour of the House of Somerset, from which he was descended, and now held by Major Michael Roger Trappes-Lomax.

Lancaster, an office which takes its name from the Lancaster, or Red Rose, branch of the Plantagenets. The title was first used by Henry IV, who was himself

Somerset Herald

formerly Duke of Lancaster. He appointed a Lancaster King of Arms, but the post was abolished by the Yorkist Edward IV. It was revived as Lancaster Herald by Henry VII. The occupant is Mr. Archibald Blomefield Russell, C.V.O., F.S.A.

Richmond, permanently established by Henry VII,

who before his accession to the throne was Duke of Richmond. The present holder is Mr. Anthony Richard Wagner.

Lancaster Herald

York, an office named after the White Rose branch of the Plantagenets, and probably created by Edward IV when he abolished the Lancaster King of Arms. The present occupant is Mr. Aubrey John Toppin, M.V.O., F.S.A.

The Pursuivants are junior to the heralds, the name meaning follower or attendant. These four officials are:

Rouge Croix (Red Cross), a name taken from the colour of the St. George's Cross, and an office created by Henry V. The present holder is Mr. John Riddell Bromhead Walker, M.C.

Rouge Dragon

Bluemantle, which probably derives from the colour of the Garter. This office is thought to have been founded by Edward III, and is now held by Mr. James Arnold Frere.

Portcullis, a name taken from one of the cognizances or badges of the House of Somerset, a favourite token of

Henry VII, by whom the office was instituted. The present occupant is the Master of Sinclair, Major Charles Murray Kennedy St. Clair, son of Lord Sinclair.

Lyon King of Arms

Rouge Dragon, an office created by Henry VII to commemorate the Red Dragon of Wales banner, which he bore at the Battle of Bosworth, where he gained the throne. Capt. Robin Ian Mirrlees was appointed last year.

The office of Bath King of Arms was instituted with the Order of the Bath in 1725 by George I. The Queen in March 1952 appointed Air Chief Marshal Sir James Robb to this position.

In Scotland there is no corporation or college of heralds. The Lord Lyon, or *Lyon King of Arms*, is an autocrat on all heraldic matters north of the Tweed, and he is independent of the jurisdiction of the Earl Marshal. Since 1871 the court of Lyon King of Arms, H.M. Register House, Edinburgh, has been a Government office. The present holder is Sir Thomas Innes of Learney, K.C.V.O., under whom are three heralds and three pursuivants. The heralds are Albany (Sir Francis James Grant, K.C.V.O.), Rothesay (Lt.-Col. H. A. B. Lawson), and Marchmont (Lt.-Col. John William Balfour Paul, D.S.O.).

The pursuivants are Dingwall (Major Charles Ian Fraser of Reelig), Unicorn (Lt.-Col. Gordon Dalyell of The Binns, C.I.E.), and Carrick (Mr. James Monteith Grant).

COLOBIUM SINDONIS. The first of the vestments in which the Queen is invested after she has been anointed. It somewhat resembles the white surplice worn by a choirboy. It is made of fine white cambric without sleeves, bordered with fine Flanders lace around the neck, shoulders, and sides. In its origin the Colobium Sindonis, which means "muslin under-garment", is an ecclesiastical garment. It corresponds with the vestment worn by a priest known as the alb.

CORNWALL, DUKE OF. This title belongs to the eldest son of the Sovereign and falls to him automatically either at his birth, if his parent is at that time Sovereign, or at the time of his parent's accession to the throne. This is the most ancient title among the dukedoms of England. Edward the Black Prince, son of King Edward III, was created first Duke of Cornwall in 1337. Under the terms of the creation the dukedom merges in the Crown when there is no heir apparent. On the death of the eldest son of the Sovereign without issue the second son inherits the dukedom, but should the first son have left issue, then the dukedom would revert to the Crown. King George III, though Prince of Wales for nine years before he succeeded his grandfather, King George II, held the Dukedom of Cornwall only from the time he ascended the throne until the birth of his eldest son.

Prince Charles, on becoming Heir Apparent on February 6, 1952, at the age of three years two months, also became Duke of Cornwall. At the same time he automatically assumed the Scottish titles of the Heir Apparent, which were brought to the Royal House of the United Kingdom by James VI of Scotland when he became James I of the United Kingdom. These titles of the eldest son of the King of Scotland, conferred in 1469, are: Duke of Rothesay, Earl of Carrick, Baron of Renfrew, Lord of the Isles and Prince and Great Steward of Scotland.

Parliament decided last year that the net revenues of the Duchy of Cornwall should be applied during the Duke's minority to the relief of the Civil List, the annual income granted to the Queen to meet personal expenses and maintain the Royal Household. But a prior annual charge of one-ninth will be devoted to the Duke of Cornwall's maintenance and education and the accumulation of a moderate capital sum on his majority. This charge represents £150,000 until his eighteenth birthday. In the last three years of his minority he will receive a further £30,000 a year.

CORONATION. The act of crowning as a ceremonial of investing a sovereign in that high office is of very great antiquity. The kings of ancient Egypt are known to have been crowned over six thousand years ago. The crowning of the kings in England has a history which goes back beyond the union of the country into one kingdom, before the times of Edward the Saxon King of Wessex and of Alfred the Great. Many of the Saxon Kings of England were crowned at the Surrey town of Kingston-on-Thames (King's Town), and the ancient Coronation Stone is still to be seen there. Since the time of William the Conqueror our kings have been crowned in Westminster Abbey. Two alone were not crowned—King Edward VIII and the young Edward V, who can scarcely be said to have reigned at all; he is supposed to have been murdered in the Tower of London by his uncle, King Richard III. One prince was crowned but never reigned—Henry, eldest son of King Henry II. The King was determined that his son should have a peaceful succession to the throne, and so had him crowned in the Abbey in 1170 by the Archbishop of York. The young man, however, died before his father, and the premature crowning served only to accentuate the quarrel between the King and Archbishop Thomas à Becket, who was murdered at Canterbury not very long afterwards.

The Coronation Service is conducted by the Archbishop of Canterbury (now Dr. Geoffrey Francis Fisher), who is assisted by the Dean of Westminster (Dr. Alan Campbell Don). It is the Archbishop who places the Crown of St. Edward upon the

Baron's Coronet Viscount's Coronet

Sovereign's head. Before he does so the Crown is placed upon the Altar and the Primate asks the following blessing:

> "O God, the Crown of the faithful: Bless we beseech Thee and sanctify this Thy servant Elizabeth our Queen: and as Thou dost this day set a Crown of pure gold upon her head, so enrich her royal heart with Thine abundant grace, and crown her with all princely virtues, through the King eternal Jesus Christ our Lord. Amen."

Then the Crown is handed by the Dean to the Archbishop, who places it upon the Queen's head. The congregation in the Abbey raise their acclamation, and "God Save the Queen!" rings out again and again. The peers and peeresses put on their coronets, the Kings of Arms their coronets. The trumpets sound a fanfare.

In former times most of the kings of Europe were crowned, but the custom has passed out of favour in other countries. The only sovereign besides our own now crowned is the King of Norway. When King Gustav V of Sweden succeeded to his throne in 1907 he decided not to be crowned on the ground that the coronation ceremony was not in accordance with the spirit of the age. A hundred years ago our King William IV suggested as a means of economy that the coronation ceremony should be abandoned, but he did not enforce the idea, although he economized very considerably in the expenditure on the ceremony.

CORONET. A kind of lesser crown worn by peers and peeresses. Coronets are made of silver gilt, with caps of crimson velvet turned up with ermine, and on the top a gold tassel.

Earl's Coronet Duke's Coronet

They are made to vary according to the rank of the wearer. The coronet of a baron has a circle of six silver balls. For a viscount the silver balls are sixteen in number. An earl is betokened by a circle with eight silver balls raised on points, with eight strawberry leaves between the points. A marquess has four gold strawberry leaves, alternating with four silver balls on points a little raised. A Duke's coronet has eight strawberry leaves.

COURT OF CLAIMS. A tribunal set up for each Coronation to decide upon the merits of the claims of various persons to render various services and perform various duties at the Coronation service. For 600 years and more these Courts have been appointed to adjudicate between rival claimants, the first recorded instance being in 1377 when John of Gaunt, "time-honoured Lancaster", sat in the White Hall of the King's

Palace of Westminster, to hear petitions arising out of the Coronation of Richard II.

In preparation for the pending Coronation, claims were heard by the Commission presided over by the Lord Chancellor, Lord Simonds. The following claims were allowed:

DEAN AND CHAPTER OF WESTMINSTER ABBEY.—To instruct the Queen in the Rites and Ceremonies and to assist the Archbishop of Canterbury and, subject to the Queen's sanction, to retain the Robes and Ornaments of the Coronation in the vestry of the Collegiate Church of St. Peter in Westminster.

BISHOP OF DURHAM AND BISHOP OF BATH AND WELLS.—To support Her Majesty at the Coronation, and to have certain privileges.

LORD DUDHOPE.—To carry the Royal Standard of Scotland as Hereditary Royal Standard Bearer for Scotland.

BARONS OF THE CINQUE PORTS.—To bear the Canopies if used in the Procession in Westminster Abbey, or, if Canopies are not used, to be assigned to a station within the Abbey in attendance upon the Queen, their ancient privileges to remain undisturbed.

THE WALKER TRUSTEES.—To be present by deputy within Westminster Abbey at the Coronation by virtue of the office of Hereditary Usher of the White Rod, or Principal Usher for Scotland.

THE CLERK OF THE CROWN.—To record the proceedings in Westminster Abbey and to be assigned a suitable place therein to discharge his duties, and that the Registrar of the Privy Council may be associated with, and assistant to, the Clerk for this purpose. Also to have five yards of scarlet cloth.

LADY ERROLL.—To be permitted to take part by deputy as Lord High Constable of Scotland, and to have a silver baton or staff, of twelve ounces weight, tipped with gold at each end, with Her Majesty's Royal Arms on one end and the Petitioner's on the other end.

LYON KING OF ARMS, HERALDS AND PURSUIVANTS OF SCOTLAND.—To be assigned usual places at the Coronation.

EARL OF SHREWSBURY.—To carry a white wand as a symbol of his office of Lord High Steward of Ireland.

MAYOR AND COMMONALTY AND CITIZENS OF THE CITY OF LONDON.—For the Lord Mayor to attend the Queen in Westminster Abbey during the Coronation, and bear the Crystal Mace.

LORD HASTINGS AND LORD CHURSTON.—To carry the great spurs.

LORD CHOLMONDELEY.—To perform and execute the duties and services of the office of Lord Great Chamberlain.

CROWNS.

Crown of England. Is placed upon the Sovereign's head during the Coronation service and is otherwise known as St. Edward's Crown—that is, the Crown of Edward the Confessor. Although it is not the same, it bears the name of the crown which was destroyed during the Commonwealth (*see* REGALIA) and which was reputed to have been the very crown with which Alfred the Great, then a child of five, was crowned by Pope Leo at Rome in the year 853. The present Crown of England was made after the Restoration for the crowning of Charles II, though it has been altered from time to time. It has encircled the brows of twelve of the fifteen sovereigns since the Restoration. The first exception was inevitable—that of Mary, wife of William of Orange. William and Mary sat upon the throne of England not as King and Consort but as sovereigns of equal right. At the coronation two crowns were needed. King William was crowned with St. Edward's Crown, and Queen Mary with the crown which had been used for Mary of Modena, consort of James II. The second exception was that of Queen Victoria. It was the size of St. Edward's Crown which led to the breach with tradition, for the crown that had been made to fit over the wig of Charles II could scarcely have been worn by the girl Queen. St. Edward's Crown on that occasion was carried in the procession of the Regalia, but was not otherwise employed. The third exception was Edward VIII, who was never crowned. If the Victorian precedent is followed there will now be a fourth exception.

The Crown consists of a circlet of gold studded with diamonds, rubies, emeralds, sapphires, and pearls. From the upper rim rise a series of ornamentations—fleur-de-lis and Cross paté. Over the top rise two golden arches, indications of a hereditary and independent monarchy. The arches at the

Crown of England

centre fall, or are depressed. This is a token that it is a royal and not an imperial crown. At the point where the arches intercept there is an orb of gold, and standing on the orb is a cross. Inside the Crown, to protect the head from the metal, is a cap of maintenance of purple velvet, trimmed with ermine. St. Edward's Crown is made of gold and is thus easily to be distinguished from the

Imperial State Crown. The personal crown of the

Sovereign, which is of silver. The use of a second crown was rendered necessary in olden times by the fact that the Crown of England was jealously guarded and for safe keeping was placed among the royal treasures in Westminster Abbey. Our Norman kings were accustomed to wear a crown on State

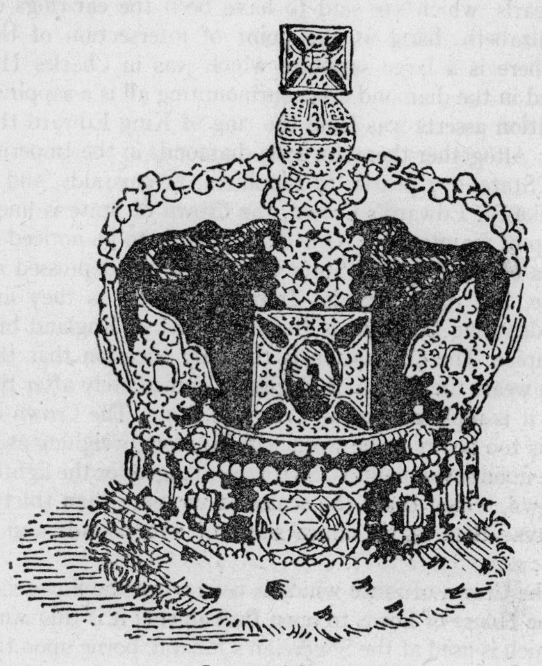

Imperial State Crown

occasions and high festivals, and as they moved about the country from place to place they needed a crown which they could carry with them ready for use as the occasion of a ceremonial might require. So they had an Imperial Crown of State constructed. The State Crown has been frequently reconstructed to suit the taste of successive wearers. The last time it was refashioned was by order of Queen Victoria, one hundred years ago. Since then it has only been dismantled and cleaned and the stones reset. The jewels with which it is adorned are of much greater value than those in St. Edward's Crown. They include the Second Star of Africa, the third largest diamond in existence, which was cut from the Cullinan diamond. Displayed above it is the Black Prince's ruby. Pear-shaped pearls, which are said to have been the ear-rings of Queen Elizabeth, hang at the point of intersection of the arches. There is a large sapphire which was in Charles II's crown, and in the diamond cross surmounting all is a sapphire that tradition asserts was from the ring of King Edward the Confessor. Altogether there are 2783 diamonds in the Imperial Crown of State, 277 pearls, 17 sapphires, 11 emeralds, and 5 rubies. Like St. Edward's Crown, the Crown of State is lined with a cap of maintenance. One distinction is to be noticed—the arches of the Imperial State Crown are not depressed at the centre, but rise upwards—Imperial arches, as they are termed—denoting that this is the crown not of England but of an Empire. The Coronation is the only occasion that the Sovereign wears the Crown of England. Immediately after the crowning it is replaced by the Crown of State. The Crown of England is too heavy to be worn with comfort, weighing as it does close upon seven pounds. So it is exchanged for the lighter State Crown, which turns the scales at no more than thirty-nine ounces—that is, an ounce short of two pounds and a half.

It is the Crown of State which is used when the Sovereign goes to the House of Lords to open Parliament; it is this same Crown which is used at the Sovereign's funeral, borne upon the coffin. In accordance with custom it stood upon the coffin of King George V as he was borne back through the streets of his capital for the last time, so that his people might pay their tribute of respect to a beloved Sovereign in Westminster Hall. On the way from King's Cross Station to Westminster the Maltese Cross which surmounts the Crown was detached from its setting by the jolting of the gun-carriage over the uneven streets. The cross fell to the ground and might have been lost for ever, but fortunately keen eyes noticed the loss and a lieutenant of the Grenadier Guards retrieved it from the roadway, carrying it for the remainder of the way to Westminster Hall.

The Crown of India was the most recently made. It was specially constructed for King George V when he travelled out to the East to be crowned Emperor of India at the Durbar at

Crown of India

Delhi in 1911. There is an ancient law which provides that the Crown of England may not be taken out of the country. So King George gave orders that a new crown should be constructed, and no less a sum than £70,000 was spent on producing a crown which should be worthy of the occasion. No fewer than 6000 precious stones are displayed on this Crown, most of them diamonds. The form is somewhat similar to the Imperial

Crown of State, but the general effect is one of greater lightness and grace. Intersecting arches rise from the circlet supporting an orb of diamonds, on which stands a cross. There is a suggestion of the Orient in the use of a lotus-flower as a decoration for the feet of the arches in place of the fleur-de-lis.

Queen Mary's Crown

Queen Mary's Crown was specially made for her use at the Coronation in 1911. This Crown is notable in that diamonds only were used for its decoration. It contains three notable gems. In the front is the Koh-i-Noor, below which is the Fourth Star of Africa, cut from the Cullinan diamond. Above, in the cross surmounting the orb, is the pear-shaped Third Star of Africa. The arches which support the orb were made so that they could easily be removed on occasions when Queen

Mary wore her crown as an open circlet at Courts and State Openings of Parliament.

There are three other crowns in the Regalia:

The Crown of Mary of Modena, consort of James II. This was used for the crowning of Queen Mary, who shared

Mary of Modena's Crown

the throne with William III. It is not of such beauty and magnificence as the others. No stones of colour adorn it, but only pearls and diamonds.

Mary of Modena's diadem, without arches, is a splendid object of its kind. No less than £110,000—an enormous sum in those days—was expended on its construction. In fact, there was a considerable criticism of King James for the manner in which he spent his money. In order to save expenditure, he abandoned the procession from the Tower of London to the Abbey, which had delighted the people on previous occasions. Twice the amount which he saved by depriving his subjects of their show was spent upon the adornment of his queen.

The Prince of Wales's Crown is the seventh in the Regalia. It is made of plain gold entirely, without a jewel in its construction, but having imitation clusters of gems and pearls carved in gold. Before the Restoration there was only a

Mary of Modena's Diadem

coronet for the use of the Prince of Wales, but Charles II ordered that an arch should be added, surmounted by the customary orb and cross. It is strange that King Charles should have made this innovation for a Prince of Wales, seeing that he had no legitimate son to hold the title.

CULLINAN DIAMOND. When uncut it was the largest diamond in the world; it produced several great gems that now ornament objects of the Regalia. The Cullinan weighed no less than 3025 carats, or one and a half pounds, when it was first placed upon the scales, following its chance discovery in a rock to the north-west of Pretoria one January day in the year 1905.

The finding was due to the sharp eyes of Captain M. F.

Wells, who was going his rounds as manager of the Premier Mine, which had been opened only two years previously. The gleam of a bright flash of light from a wall of yellow ground eighteen feet below the surface was the clue which resulted in the great stone being brought to view. It received its name from the chairman of the mining company, Sir Thomas Cullinan.

England and her sovereigns are indebted to the two great South African warrior statesmen, General Botha and General Smuts, for the thought which led to the Cullinan being presented to King Edward VII two years afterwards. These two South Africans, who had fought against England in the Boer War, were striving for the betterment of relations between their Union and the Motherland. What better token, they thought, could there be of South Africa's loyalty to the Crown than to present the greatest jewel in the world to the occupant of the Imperial Throne? The idea thus happily conceived was carried out thanks to the generosity of the Government of the Transvaal, which bought the stone for the sum of £150,000 and presented it to King Edward on his sixty-sixth birthday, November 9, 1907. In a happily phrased message the hope was expressed that the gem, representing a Greater South Africa, would become one of the brightest jewels in the British Crown.

Curtana

The Cullinan diamond as a single entity does not exist today. It was cleaved and cut at Amsterdam into nine larger and ninety-six smaller brilliants. The largest of these bear the name of Stars of South Africa. The principal stones and their weights are:

		Weight
Great Star of Africa, in the Sceptre .		516½ carats
Second Star of Africa, in the Crown of State		309 ,,
Third Star of Africa	Both in Queen Mary's Crown	92 ,,
Fourth Star of Africa		62 ,,

CURTANA, or Sword of Mercy. One of a set of three swords made by order of King Charles II from ancient drawings of the three swords given by the Pope to King Henry VIII. The swords are of exactly the same pattern, straight with broad blades, but the Curtana has a blunt point, six inches of the blade having been purposely broken off. This shortening and breaking of the point was designed to indicate Mercy. It is carried in the Coronation procession by one of the peers.

D

DECLARATION of the Protestant Faith is required to be made by each new sovereign. It is in the following words:

> "I do solemnly and sincerely in the presence of God confess, testify, and declare that I am a faithful Protestant, and that I will, according to the true intent of the enactments which secure the Protestant succession to the Throne of my realm, uphold and maintain the said enactments to the best of my powers according to law."

DURHAM, BISHOP OF. By ancient privilege attends the Sovereign throughout the Coronation, standing at her right hand as a supporter, the Bishop of Bath and Wells being on the left. The Rt. Rev. Arthur Michael Ramsey, forty-eight, was appointed to the See a year ago after being Regius Professor of Divinity at Cambridge.

E

EARL MARSHAL. High official of the Court responsible for the ordering of great ceremonies of State, who thus makes the arrangements for the Coronation. The office is held by the Duke of Norfolk, having been associated with the title of Norfolk for nearly 500 years. It is the Earl Marshal who issues

Earl Marshal in uniform

details of the order of ceremonial and instructions for the robes to be worn by peers and peeresses and others. On the day itself he and his assistants marshal—that is to say, direct—arrivals and departures of the Sovereign, her attendants, and the distinguished company at Westminster Abbey. He is assisted by members of the College of Arms, or Heralds'

College, of which he is the head. The office of Earl Marshal is an hereditary one, having passed from father to son in four families with which it has been associated since the first creation of the office by King Stephen in the year 1135. It was conferred upon John Howard, ancestor of the present Duke of Norfolk, in the year 1483, and has continued in the family from that date to the present day, except that at various periods it was forfeited in troublous times, but it was afterwards restored. The father of the present Duke carried out the arrangements for the Coronation of King Edward VII and King George V. The present, and sixteenth, holder of the Dukedom, Bernard Marmaduke Fitzalan-Howard, was born in 1908 and succeeded his father at the age of nine. He married the Hon. Lavinia Strutt in 1937. The Duke of Norfolk is Premier Duke of England. He also holds the subsidiary titles of Earl of Arundel, Baron Maltravers, Baron Fitzalan of Clun and Oswaldestre, Baron Herries and Earl of Norfolk. He is the owner of the magnificent Sussex Castle of Arundel.

He was in charge of the arrangements at the funeral of George V, the Coronation of George VI and the funeral of George VI. He and his staff have devoted months of planning to the arrangements for Queen Elizabeth's Coronation day and the complicated ceremonials.

ELIZABETH I, daughter of King Henry VIII and his second wife Anne Boleyn. Born at Greenwich, September 7, 1533, she succeeded her half-sister, Queen Mary Tudor, in 1558 and was crowned Queen of "England, France and Ireland" on January 15, 1559. After a long and illustrious reign she died at the Royal Palace of Sheen, Richmond, on March 24, 1603. She was unmarried, the only adult sovereign of England not married until King Edward VIII. The Tudor dynasty ended with her and she was succeeded by the first of the Stuarts, King James I of England and VI of Scotland.

ELIZABETH II, sixth Queen in her own right and forty-first sovereign of England since the Norman Conquest. Born April 21, 1926, daughter of King George VI and Queen Elizabeth; succeeded her father February 6, 1952. (*See* ROYAL FAMILY.)

ERMINE. Fur used for robes of peers and peeresses made from the pure white winter coat of the stoat with the black tips of the tails arranged at regular intervals to form a series of black points. The arrangement of the ermine on the robes denotes the rank of the wearer. Two rows of ermine is the token of a baron, two and a half of a viscount, three rows of an earl, three and a half that of a marquess, and four rows that of a duke.

F

FEALTY. The act of acknowledging fidelity to the newly crowned Sovereign by the Bishops before the peers do homage. (*See* HOMAGE.)

G

GARTER. Order of Knighthood, the members of which take part in the Coronation ceremonial. Four Knights of the Garter hold over the Queen a rich pall of silk or cloth-of-gold as she sits in King Edward's Chair for her anointing and investiture. Founded by King Edward III in 1348, the Order consists of the Sovereign and twenty-five Knight Companions with the addition of members of the Royal Family and extra Knights by special statute. The habit and ensigns of the Order are: (1) A Garter of dark-blue velvet edged with gold, bearing the motto "*Honi soit qui mal y pense*" in golden letters, with buckle and pendant of gold, which is worn on the left leg below the knee. (2) A Mantle of blue velvet, lined with taffeta, with the Star of the Order embroidered on the left breast. (3) A Hood of crimson velvet. (4) A Surcoat of crimson velvet lined with white taffeta. (5) A black velvet Hat lined with white taffeta, fastened by a band of diamonds, a plume of white ostrich feathers, in the centre of which is a tuft of black heron's feathers. (6) A Collar of gold consisting of twenty-six garters, enamelled blue, each enclosing a red rose. (7) The George, an enamelled figure of St. George on horseback en-

Knight of the Garter in full habit

countering the dragon. (8) The Lesser George, worn on a broad dark-blue ribbon over the left shoulder. (8) The Star of eight points of silver, upon the centre of which is the Cross of St. George encircled with the garter. The Prelate of the Order is always the Bishop of Winchester. At his investiture a Knight is allotted a stall in St. George's Chapel, Windsor, over which is set up, to be retained for his life, his sword, helmet, crest, banner, and a plate containing his arms and titles.

Gentleman-at-arms

GENTLEMEN-AT-ARMS. The full title is the Queen's Body Guard of the Honourable Corps of Gentlemen-at-Arms. It was instituted as a body of Gentleman Pensioners in 1509 by Henry VIII, who wished to rival his father's creation of another royal bodyguard, the Yeomen of the Guard.

In addition to their duties at royal ceremonies and processions, the Gentlemen-at-Arms, with their Standard Bearer on one side and their Lieutenant on the other, usually walk on the left and right of the Sovereign in the Coronation procession within Westminster Abbey. The Captain walks in the rear of the Sovereign and by the side of the Captain of the Yeomen of the Guard. In 1851 the privileges of the Hon. Corps of Gentlemen-at-Arms as the first bodyguard of the Sovereign

St. George (as he appears on the Garter Badge)

were defined by order of Queen Victoria. (*See also* YEOMEN OF THE GUARD.)

GEORGE. The name of England's patron saint, and of six of our Sovereigns, is derived from a Greek word which means husbandman or farmer. Historians do not agree exactly who was the person now revered as St. George. The most commonly accepted story is that he was born in Armorica, and was beheaded on April 23 in the year 303 during the persecution of the Christians under the Roman Emperor Diocletian. In the next century many churches were erected in his honour. According to the old English poem which describes the dragon-killing feat, St. George was the son of Lord Albert of Coventry. When he grew up he fought against the Saracens. In Libya he heard of a huge dragon to which every day a girl was given for food. When he went to kill the dragon, the girl chosen for sacrifice was Sabra, the King's daughter. She was tied to the stake and the dragon was approaching. St. George rode up, thrust his lance into the monster's mouth, and killed it on the spot. St. George brought Sabra to England as his wife, and they lived happily at Coventry. The saint's first connection with England is traced back to the time of King Arthur in the sixth century, who placed the picture of St. George on his banners. It is asserted that George was the patron saint of England in Saxon times. In the year 1222 it was commanded that his festival should be observed in England as a holiday of lesser rank. In 1344 the saint was adopted as patron of the Order of the Garter.

GEORGE VI. Father of Queen Elizabeth, thirty-fifth King and the fortieth Sovereign of England since the Norman Conquest. He was the third Sovereign of the House of Windsor, but the first of the House of Windsor to be crowned as such. As Duke of York, he succeeded to the throne on the abdication of his brother King Edward VIII. Other Dukes of York who have succeeded to the throne were Edward IV, Henry VIII, Charles I, James II, and George V. He was the fifth King to succeed his brother, the others being Henry I, brother of William Rufus; John, brother of Richard I; James II, brother of Charles II; and William IV, brother of George IV. Since William and Mary were crowned after the flight of James II, George VI was the first Sovereign to be crowned during the lifetime of his predecessor. When he was born on December 14, 1895, at York Cottage, Sandringham, second son of the Duke and Duchess of York, afterwards George V and Queen Mary, there seemed little likelihood that he would ever be King. He was christened Albert Frederick Arthur George and was known as Prince Albert. He was eighteen months younger than his elder brother, the Prince of Wales, now the Duke of Windsor, and sixteen months older than his sister Mary, now the Princess Royal. At the age of fourteen he began his career as a sailor, entering the Royal Naval College at Osborne, Isle of Wight, and later going to Dartmouth. He served in the

Battle of Jutland in 1916 in the *Collingwood*, which came to grips with two German cruisers and a number of destroyers. For his coolness under fire in the battleship's fore-turret he was mentioned in dispatches. The ensign flown by the *Collingwood* became one of his most treasured possessions. Later he transferred to the Royal Naval Air Service, soon absorbed by the R.A.F., and gained his pilot's licence. At the end of the war Prince Albert represented King George V at the ceremonial re-entry of King Albert of the Belgians into his capital of Brussels.

In 1920 the Prince became a Cambridge undergraduate at Trinity College, studying history, economics, and political science. When twenty-four he was created Duke of York. On January 6, 1923, came the announcement of his engagement to Lady Elizabeth Bowes-Lyon, daughter of the fourteenth Earl and the Countess of Strathmore. He had proposed to her three days before while walking in the woods near St. Paul's Waldenbury, Lord Strathmore's Hertfordshire home.

They were married in Westminster Abbey on April 26, 1923, and took up residence at White Lodge, Richmond. Their marriage proved a happy partnership. In the autumn of 1924 the Duke and Duchess made their first tour abroad, visiting East Africa. Later they made their town residence at 17 Bruton Street, Mayfair, London home of the Duchess's parents, and it was there, on April 21, 1926, that their first child, Princess Elizabeth, now Queen Elizabeth II, was born. That same year they moved to 145 Piccadilly—destroyed by a German bomb during the war—their London home until as King and Queen they entered into occupation of Buckingham Palace.

The Duke made history at Wimbledon in 1926. He was the first member of the Royal Family to play in the all-England tennis championships, being beaten in the first round of the men's doubles with Sir Louis Greig. A second Empire tour was made in the battle cruiser *Renown* in 1927 to New Zealand and to Australia, where the Duke opened the new Federal Parliament building at Canberra. The royal couple's second child, Princess Margaret Rose, was born on August 21, 1930, at Glamis Castle, ancestral home of her Scottish grandparents. During the succeeding years the Duke became prominently associated with industrial problems and social welfare. He was the first president of the Industrial Welfare Society and he founded the Duke of York's Camp, where boys from public schools mixed with lads from the factories and mines.

These interests which he developed as a younger son paradoxically proved an ideal preparation for the kingship to which he was to succeed in circumstances without parallel so soon after his father's death. George V died on January 21, 1936. By December 11 that same year the new King, Edward VIII, had abdicated and the Duke of York had succeeded to the throne as George VI three days before his forty-first birthday. His first act as Sovereign was to create his elder brother Duke of Windsor.

As international tension grew, the King and Queen embarked on May 6, 1939, on a royal tour unprecedented in our history. For the first time the wearer of the British Crown set foot in the United States. No reigning sovereign and his consort had ever crossed the Atlantic before or had visited Canada or any other Dominion. From coast to coast in Canada and as the guests of President Roosevelt in the United States Their Majesties received an unforgettable welcome. They returned home to a country which was preparing for the storm of 1939–45 to break.

On the evening of September 3, the day war was declared, the King made a stirring broadcast to the nation. Thereafter he and the Queen were tireless in their efforts to show that the Throne and the people were one in facing the ordeal before them. On September 13, 1940, a German 'plane bombed Buckingham Palace when the King and Queen were in residence—one of fourteen raids on the Palace—causing considerable damage. In 1943 the King flew to his troops in North Africa. Not since the Earl of Chester, later Edward I, marshalled his army in Tunisia for the crusade in 1270 had an English prince seen his forces on active service in Africa. Ten days after D-Day he was in the Normandy bridgehead. He later visited the troops in Italy and the advancing Allied

Army in Holland and Belgium. Outstanding post-war events were the Royal Family's South African visit in 1947 and Princess Elizabeth's engagement and marriage to the Duke of

Gold Stick

Edinburgh later the same year. In the following year Their Majesties celebrated their silver wedding and 4000 people thronged St. Paul's for the thanksgiving service. Upon this domestic happiness the seal was set by the birth on November 14, 1948, of Prince Charles.

But that same month the King was stricken. It was announced that he was suffering from obstruction to the circulation in the legs and his projected tour of Australia and

Silver Stick

New Zealand was put off. Early in 1949 an operation was performed. On May 3, 1951, His Majesty opened the Festival of Britain, toured the Exhibition next day and attended the inaugural concert in the Royal Festival Hall. These were his last important public appearances. In September a lung operation was carried out. It was arranged that Princess Elizabeth should make the visit to Australia and New Zealand in his place. The end came suddenly. Six days after he had bid good-bye to Princess Elizabeth on her departure from London Airport he died in his sleep peacefully at Sandringham on February 6, 1952. At the lying-in-state at Westminster Hall 305,806 of his subjects filed past in three days.

GLOUCESTER, DUKE OF, uncle of Queen Elizabeth, son of King George V, born Sandringham, March 31, 1900. (*See under* ROYAL FAMILY.)

GOLD STICKS. Like Black Rod, this office gets its name from the holder's baton. Charles II originated the post, which is now held by the honorary colonels of the regiments of Household Cavalry—the Earl of Athlone, Queen Mary's brother (Life Guards), and Major-Gen. Sir Richard Howard-Vyse (Royal Horse Guards)—in rotation for periods of a month. At the Coronation and other State functions Gold Stick walks close behind the Queen. In the Coronation procession within Westminster Abbey Gold Stick usually has the Master of the Household on one hand and the Master of the Horse on his other. The Captain of the Honourable Corps of Gentlemen-at-Arms, Earl Fortescue, is also a Gold Stick, as is the Captain-General of the Royal Company of Archers for Scotland, Lord Elphinstone, the Queen's uncle by marriage, who appears at the Coronation as Gold Stick for Scotland. Silver Stick, also originated by Charles II, is the Colonel Commanding Household Cavalry who may be an officer of either the Life Guards or the Blues. Col. E. J. S. Wood, M.V.O., M.C. (Life Guards), is the present holder of the post. Three officers of the Gentlemen-at-Arms are Silver Sticks—the Lieutenant, the Standard Bearer, and the Clerk of the Cheque.

H

HOLYROODHOUSE, PALACE OF. This Edinburgh palace of the Scottish kings is the official royal residence in

Holyroodhouse

Scotland. It was begun about 1500 by James IV, but it is the six tragic years spent there by Mary Queen of Scots from 1561 to 1567 that have given the place its haunting air of romantic tragedy. There took place her famous interview with John Knox, the murder of Rizzio, and Mary's marriage to Bothwell. It was destroyed by fire in 1650, all but two towers, and rebuilt twenty years later.

HOMAGE. Homage is paid to the newly crowned Sovereign by peers of the realm, and the bishops do fealty to her. First to do fealty is the Archbishop of Canterbury, who kneels before Her Majesty's knees and says:

> "I will be faithful and true, and faith and truth will bear unto you, our Sovereign Lady, and your heirs Kings of Great Britain, Ireland and the British Dominions beyond the seas, Defenders of the Faith. And I will do, and truly acknowledge, the service of the lands I claim to hold of you, as in right of the Church. So help me God."

The Archbishop's words are repeated by the Bishops present, and the Archbishop kisses Her Majesty's left cheek.

After the Lords Spiritual follow the Princes of the Blood Royal.

At the Coronation of King George V the Prince of Wales pronounced the words:

> "I do become your liege man of life and limb, and of earthly worship, and faith and truth I will bear unto you, to live and die, against all manner of folks. So help me God."

The other peers of the realm then render homage, the first of each order kneeling before Her Majesty, the others kneeling in their places and repeating the words. At their head is the Duke of Norfolk, as premier duke; then should come Lord Winchester, as premier marquess, but in view of his advanced age his place may probably be taken by Lord Huntly; and next, Lord Shrewsbury, Talbot, and Waterford, as premier earl. Lord Hereford, the premier viscount, should follow, and although a minor, he may be permitted to do so according to an old precedent. Otherwise, Lord Falkland is next in seniority, but as he is unlikely to attend, his place might be taken by Lord Arbuthnott. Lastly comes the premier baron, Lord Mowbray, Segrave, and Stourton, holder of titles granted by Edward I.

The first of each order of peers then ascends to the throne, and, stretching forth his hand, touches the crown on Her Majesty's head, "as promising by that ceremony for himself and his Order to be ever ready to support it with all their power". He then kisses Her Majesty's cheek. The act of homage, under the feudal system, was one of the essential ceremonies in the granting of a fief.

I

IMPERIAL STATE CROWN. (*See* CROWNS.)

INDIA: DURBAR AND VICEROY. Durbar, from a Persian word meaning court, is the name applied to the ceremonial at which the King-Emperor was proclaimed in India. Queen Victoria, Edward VII, and George V were proclaimed at Delhi in 1877, 1903, and 1911 respectively, but only George V was actually present in person. Edward VIII and George VI were never so proclaimed, the former owing to his brief reign, and the latter owing to unsettled world conditions. Durbars and the line of Viceroys of India dating from 1858 ended with the granting of Indian independence and the establishment of the two new states of India and Pakistan on August 15, 1947. The last Viceroy,

Viscount (now Earl) Mountbatten, uncle of the Duke of Edinburgh, took over his office on March 22, 1947. On August 15 he became first Governor-General of the Dominion of India until he handed over to an Indian on June 21, 1948.

K

KENT, DUCHESS OF, aunt of Queen Elizabeth and widow of the first Duke. (*See under* ROYAL FAMILY.)

KING'S CHAMPION, or CHAMPION OF ENGLAND. The office of King's Champion originated with William the Conqueror. When the Dukes of Normandy were inaugurated, a member of a family holding the barony of Fonteney appeared as the duke's champion. And when Robert de Marmion, a member of this family, came to England with

King's Champion at the Coronation of George IV

William, he was granted English lands on the same tenure, thus becoming Hereditary Champion of England:

> Lord of Fontenaye,
> Of Lutteward and Scrivelbaye,
> Of Tamworth Tower and Town.

"Scrivelbaye" is the manor of Scrivelsby in Lincolnshire, held by grand serjeanty with the service of being the King's Champion at the Coronation. Scrivelsby passed to Sir John Dymoke, a Gloucestershire knight of the fourteenth century, by his marriage with the heiress of the Marmions, and to this day it is the Dymoke family which claims the right of hereditary championship to the Crown. The first recorded appearance of the Champion was at Richard II's coronation in 1377; his last at George IV's in 1821. In early times, it would appear, the Champion took part in the procession and made his challenge on the way to the coronation as well as after it in Westminster Hall. In 1377 the words of the Champion's challenge, proclaimed by the herald, were as follows:

> "Yf ther be any man of high degree or lowe, that will saie that this oure soverayn liege Lorde Richarde, cousin and heire of the Kynge of Englande, Edwarde late deceased, ought not of right to be Kynge of Englande crowned, he is redy now till the laste houre of his brethe, with his bodie, to bete him like a false man and a traitor, on what other daie that shal be apoynted."

In latter times the Champion rendered his service at the Coronation banquet in Westminster Hall and when the banquet was discontinued the Champion lost the occasion for his challenge. Dymoke of Scrivelsby, however, still has a rare honour at the Coronation, which is to carry the Standard of England. The present head of the family is Capt. J. L. Marmion Dymoke, serving with the Royal Lincolnshire Regiment.

What an amazing reminder of the days of chivalry and feudalism the Champion's challenge was! One looks through the mists of time and sees the Champion in white armour ride into Westminster Hall on a white horse; before him come trumpeters, serjeants-at-arms with their maces, his two esquires bearing lance and shield, and four pages. Then draws nigh the Champion himself, the Earl Marshal on his one side and the Lord High Constable on his other. Follows the challenge and the casting-down of the glove, which is retrieved by the herald. The Champion moves on and, after the challenge has been several times repeated, approaches the king's table and makes his final challenge. The royal cup-bearer hands him wine in a gilt cup. The Champion drinks to the king; the king drinks to his Champion . . . and, wheeling on his horse, the white knight rides off triumphantly bearing the cup as fee.

KISS OF HOMAGE. Given to the newly crowned sovereign by the peers of the realm. According to the historians the kiss is an essential part of the ceremony of homage, whose omission might be considered to invalidate the ceremony—"the homage hath not it seems enough of what is legal without it". In the time of Henry VI there was a Great Plague in London, and it was considered advisable, because of the risk of infection, that the kiss should be omitted. An Act of Parliament was passed to "ordain and grant that everiche of your said lieges in the doing of their said homage may omit the said kissing of you and be excused thereof (at your will the homage being of the same force as though they kissed you) and have their letters of doing their homage, the kissing of you omitted notwithstanding".

KNIGHTS OF THE BATH. A picturesque custom of the old days is held to explain the origin of the Order of Knights of the Bath. Before the sovereign left the Tower of London for his coronation in Westminster Abbey he created a number of knights to attend him at his crowning. The knight-to-be bathed and then, donning a hermit's weed, kept vigil in church. Next morning, in magnificent apparel, he received his sword and spurs, and was created knight by the king. As these knighthoods were made in time of peace, the knights were without an order. They came to be called Knights of the Bath from the circumstance of their ablutions—a symbol of purity—before their creation. Thus, according to older historians, the Order of the Bath had its origin; but modern authorities dispute the connection. They do not allow that the knights who bathed were really members of a separate order of knighthood.

At any rate in 1725 George I renewed the Order, fixing it at 37 knights and the sovereign. It was enlarged in 1815 with three classes, including civil (as well as military) Knights

Knight of the Bath

Grand Cross, and again 32 years later with the addition of civil Knights Commander and Companions. The numbers have grown since then. The officers are the Dean of Westminster, the Bath King of Arms, the Registrar and the Usher of the Scarlet Rod.

KOH-I-NOOR. One of the most famous diamonds in the world, and one of the gems in the Queen's crown. The name means "Mountain of Light". The stone has a history extending over five thousand years. It is reputed to have been found in one of the Golconda mines near the Kishna River in the State of Hyderabad, and was worn by Karna, one of the legendary heroes of the sacred book of the Hindoos. Its authentic history begins about six hundred years ago. Theft, trickery, and murder form its record until it passed into the possession of the British Crown.

It was lost to the kings of Golconda by the treachery of a general, who some time in the sixteenth century presented it to the Great Mogul. Nadir Shah, Persian conqueror of India, wrested it by a trick from the Mogul Emperor Mohammed.

Nadir had captured the entire treasure of the Moguls, this stone alone excepted. For long the secret of its whereabouts baffled him, until it was revealed by a woman of the harem. Mohammed, she declared, wore the gem in his head-dress. Nadir insisted on exchanging his turban, glittering with many gems, for the plain headgear of the Emperor, and thus at last gained the jewel, which in his delight he called "Mountain of Light". Its possession brought death to Nadir's son, and it passed to Afghan hands. Again there was a trail of suffering, and the diamond was gained by Runjeet Singh, the famous ruler of Lahore. This was the manner by which he acquired it:

> Having heard that the Khan of Kabul possessed a diamond that had belonged to the Great Mogul, the largest and purest known, he invited the unfortunate owner to his court, and there, having him in his power, demanded the diamond. The guest, however, had provided himself against such a contingency with a perfect imitation of the coveted jewel. After some show of resistance, he reluctantly acceded to the wishes of his powerful host. The delight of Runjeet was extreme, but of short duration, the lapidary to whom he gave orders to mount his new acquisition pronouncing it to be merely a bit of crystal. The mortification and rage of the despot were unbounded. He immediately ordered the palace of the Khan to be invested, and ransacked from top to bottom. For a long while, all search was vain. At last a slave betrayed the secret; the diamond was found concealed beneath a heap of ashes. Runjeet Singh had it set in an armlet, between two diamonds each the size of a sparrow's egg.

After the Mutiny, and the annexation of the Punjab, the diamond was presented to Queen Victoria. The stone that is now to be seen in the Queen's crown, magnificent though it be, is only a small part of the great gem that was once the Koh-i-Noor. Originally, we are told, it weighed 793 carats, but was reduced by an unskilled stone-cutter in India to 280 carats. When it was shown at the Great Exhibition in London in 1851 it turned the scales at 186 carats, but thereafter the jewellery experts advised that it should be reset to show it off to greater advantage. It was worked on once again by the Court jeweller. The Duke of Wellington gave the first touch to the grinding, which occupied the labours of 38 days. The gem was thus reduced to its present size of 106 carats.

L

LARDERER, CHIEF. When the coronation banquet was held in Westminster Hall the Chief Larderer was responsible for supplying the meats. As perquisite he received the meats left over at the end of the banquet.

LORD CHAMBERLAIN. The Lord Chamberlain, not to be confused with the Lord Great Chamberlain (*q.v.*), is the chief officer of the Royal Household. His jurisdiction extends, in the old phrase, to all officers and servants "above stairs". In olden time the Lord Chamberlain, then known as the King's Chamberlain, wielded great political power. Today he is concerned with a variety of important duties, among which are the ordering of State ceremonies, examining the claims of those who wish to be presented at Court, the licensing of certain theatres, the censoring of plays. At the Coronation procession within Westminster Abbey the Lord Chamberlain is attended by an officer of the Jewel House carrying the Rings and the Sword for the offering. Many officials with picturesque duties are under the Lord Chamberlain's superintendence. For example, the Serjeants-at-Arms, who attend on the Sovereign, and at the Coronation wait on the bearers of the Regalia (the Serjeants-at-Arms in the House of Commons and the House of Lords attend the Speaker and the Lord Chancellor). The Lord Chamberlain also appoints royal physicians and surgeons, the Queen's chaplains, and the royal tradesmen.

Lord Chamberlain

The present holder of the post is the Earl of Scarbrough, who was appointed to the office in succession to the Earl of Clarendon. Eleventh holder of a title created in 1690, Lord Scarbrough was formerly M.P. for York and Governor of Bombay (1937–43).

LORD CHIEF JUSTICE OF ENGLAND. When William the Conqueror came from Normandy he introduced into England the office of Chief Justiciar, who eventually

Lord Chief Justice

presided over a tribunal for the whole of the country, and whose powers, in the absence of the king, approached those of a viceroy. Ultimately, when the system grew, the Justiciar became known as Chief Justice of the King's Bench. Sir Edward Coke, who was made Chief Justice of the King's

Bench in 1613, bestowed upon himself the title of Lord Chief Justice of England, and thus it has been ever since. Lord Goddard, the present Lord Chief Justice, born 1877, was

Lord Great Chamberlain

appointed in 1946. He was educated at Marlborough and Trinity, Oxford. K.C., 1923. Recorder of Poole, 1917–25; Bath, 1925–8; Plymouth, 1928–32. High Court Judge, 1932–8. Lord Justice of Appeal, 1938–44. Lord of Appeal, 1944–6. He is the holder of a life barony and he has three daughters.

LORD GREAT CHAMBERLAIN. Not to be confused with the Lord Chamberlain, who is the chief official of the Royal Household. For this hereditary office of State there were three claimants in 1902, and when the matter was referred to the House of Lords the office was divided between the Earl of Ancaster, the Marquess of Cholmondeley, and the representatives of the Marquess of Lincolnshire. The holder of the office changes with each reigning monarch, and his duties begin immediately the new sovereign is proclaimed. Lord Cholmondeley, who was Lord Great Chamberlain during the brief time that King Edward VIII was on the throne, returned to the office with the accession of Queen Elizabeth II. He occupies the office in alternate reigns as he holds a half-moiety, and the other two a quarter each. At the Coronation ceremony the Lord Great Chamberlain stands on the left of the Queen, fastens the mantle after investiture, and finally places on her the purple robes. When the monarch opens Parliament in person the Lord Great Chamberlain is in attendance.

LORD HIGH CHANCELLOR. The Lord High Chancellor, whose salary is £10,000 a year, is the Keeper of the Great Seal, the delivery of which to his charge signifies his appointment. He is the chief Judge in England and adviser to the Crown on legal matters, and he appoints Judges of the Court of Appeal, the High Court, and the County Courts, as well as Justices of the Peace. His is a political appointment—he has a seat in the Cabinet—for the Lord Chancellor resigns with his party. In the table of precedence he ranks above all dukes not of the Blood Royal, and next to the Archbishop of Canterbury; he is the second peer in the kingdom. In the House of Lords he sits on the Woolsack, acting as Speaker. The present Lord Chancellor, Lord Simonds, was appointed on the formation of Mr. Churchill's Government after the General Election in October 1951. Born on November 28, 1881, he was educated at Winchester and New College, Oxford. Called to the Bar at Lincoln's Inn, 1906; took silk, 1924; appointed to the Bench and knighted, 1937; Lord of Appeal, 1944.

LORD HIGH CONSTABLE. The office of Lord High Constable, one of the four great officers at the Coronation ceremony, was hereditary until 1521, when Henry VIII abolished it. Like the Lord High Stewardship, it is revived only for special occasions. The great Duke of Wellington held this office at three coronations—those of George IV, William IV, and Queen Victoria. The duties of the High Constable are to attend the monarch and to assist at the reception of the Regalia. The Marquess of Crewe was Lord High Constable at the last Coronation.

LORD HIGH CONSTABLE OF SCOTLAND. By hereditary right the holder of the Earldom of Erroll walks as Lord High Constable of Scotland at the Coronation, carrying a silver staff weighing twelve ounces tipped with gold at each end, with the Sovereign's arms on one end and those of the Earls of Erroll on the other. The present and twenty-eighth Hereditary Lord High Constable of Scotland is a woman, the Countess of Erroll, who succeeded her father, the twenty-second Earl, in 1941 at the age of fifteen. She married Captain Iain Moncreiffe, Scots Guards, in 1946 and has one son. The Court of Claims decided that Lady Erroll's duties should be carried out by a deputy to be approved by the Queen.

LORD HIGH STEWARD. One of the four great officers of State at the Coronation ceremony. The others are the Lord Great Chamberlain, the Lord High Constable, and the Earl Marshal. In Anglo-Saxon England the Lord High Steward, the *steadward* or ward of the king's "place", was what may be described as the sovereign's deputy or viceroy. When Richard II was crowned, John of Gaunt was Lord High Steward by hereditary right. However, when his own son ascended the throne as Henry IV, the office was embodied in the Crown; it was too powerful an office to be held by one man. Since then it has been revived only for limited periods during special occasions, chief of which are coronations and trials of peers. At the Coronation the Lord High Steward, by ancient right, walks before the sovereign and carries the Crown of St. Edward. The fourth Marquess of Salisbury, father of the present peer, performed this office at the Coronation of King George VI.

LORD HIGH STEWARD OF IRELAND. An office

created in the fifteenth century. The Earl of Shrewsbury, who attends the Coronation in this capacity, carries a white wand as symbol of his office. The present Lord Shrewsbury, the twenty-first, who is premier Earl of England, was born in 1914.

Lord Mayor with the crystal mace

LORD MAYOR OF LONDON. In the Coronation procession the Lord Mayor of London, representing the commonalty and citizens of the City of London, walks on the left of Garter King of Arms, with the Gentleman Usher of the Black Rod on the right. Dressed in his robes of office, he carries the crystal mace. At one time the Lord Mayor and twelve representatives of the commonalty of London were permitted to assist the Chief Butler. The Mayor, Bailiffs, and Commonalty of Oxford once had a like privilege. The title of Lord Mayor of London goes back to the reign of Edward III; previously the title was Mayor. The Coronation Lord Mayor is Sir Rupert De la Bère, Conservative M.P. for South Worcestershire.

LORD PRIVY SEAL. Has custody of the Privy Seal, which must be affixed on the warrant of the sovereign to charters, pardons, and other documents before they are passed for the Great Seal, which is in the custody of the Lord Chancellor. Nowadays the Lord Privy Seal is a member of the Cabinet. The present holder of the office, appointed on May 7, 1952, is Mr. Harry Crookshank, who combines it with Leader of the House of Commons in Mr. Churchill's Government. Conservative M.P. for Gainsborough since 1924, and before that a member of the Diplomatic Service, he has held several important ministerial posts. Born in Cairo on May 27, 1893, he was educated at Eton, where he was a King's Scholar, and at Magdalen, Oxford. He served with the Grenadier Guards in the First World War.

LORD STEWARD, THE. The Lord Steward of the Royal Household is the second great officer at Court, the first being the Lord Chamberlain. He has been described as having authority "below stairs", when in charge of officers and servants who did not come under the superintendence of the Lord Chamberlain. His office is formally styled the Board of the Green Cloth. The Duke of Hamilton and Brandon has occupied this office since 1937. He was born on February 3, 1903, and was previously known as the boxing Marquess of Clydesdale. Hereditary Keeper of the Palace of Holyroodhouse, he is a Douglas who married a Percy, Lady Elizabeth Percy, daughter of the eighth Duke of Northumberland, in 1937. Chief Pilot of the Everest Flight Expedition in 1933, he served in the R.A.F. during the war as Group Captain and Air Commodore.

M

MARGARET, PRINCESS, sister of Queen Elizabeth and second daughter of King George VI, born Glamis Castle, August 21, 1930. (*See under* ROYAL FAMILY.)

MARLBOROUGH HOUSE. Home of Queen Mary since the death of George V in 1936, Marlborough House, overlooking the Mall, was built by Christopher Wren in

Marlborough House

1709–10 for the great Duke of Marlborough, Mr. Churchill's famous ancestor. It was the dowager house of Queen Adelaide, widow of William IV, town residence of two Princes of Wales, Edward VII and George V, until their accession, and the home of the widowed Queen Alexandra.

MARY, QUEEN, grandmother of Queen Elizabeth and widow of King George V; born Kensington Palace, May 26, 1867, daughter of the Duke and Duchess of Teck. (*See under* ROYAL FAMILY.)

MASTER OF THE HORSE. After the Lord Chamberlain and the Lord Steward, the third great officer of the Royal Household is the Master of the Horse, who in royal processions has the place behind the Sovereign. As his title suggests, he has charge of the royal stables. The Duke of Beaufort, the present Master of the Horse, was appointed by King Edward VIII in July 1936, succeeding the Earl of Granard.

MASTER OF THE QUEEN'S MUSICK. This office was created by the Merry Monarch, Charles II, at the Restoration in 1660 to provide music for the Court. Nowadays the duties are advisory—on music for royal ceremonies. Sir Arnold Bax, the twenty-first holder of this coveted post, was appointed in 1942. His predecessors were Sir Walford Davies and Sir Edward Elgar. He wrote the fanfares sounded at the wedding of the Queen to the Duke of Edinburgh in 1947. The Funeral March which he composed for the film *Malta, G.C.*, during the war, was played at the funeral service for George VI at St. George's Chapel, Windsor. Sir Arnold was born on November 6, 1883, and was knighted in 1937.

N

NATIONAL ANTHEM. After 51 years the National Anthem is again "God Save the Queen". In his notable broadcast the night after the death of King George VI, Mr. Churchill, after a characteristic passage in which he welcomed the new Elizabethan age—"Famous have been the reigns of our Queens"—concluded with these words: "I, whose youth was passed in the august, unchallenged and tranquil glories of the Victorian era, may well feel a thrill in invoking once more the prayer and the anthem 'God Save the Queen'." There has been much controversy and little light on the authorship of the anthem. It is said to have been first sung as his own composition—words and music—by Henry Cary in 1740. An earlier form of the air in 1619 is attributed to John Bull, who has long been credited with the origin of the anthem. Cary and Bull are generally thought to share the credit, but a strong candidate is James Oswald, a Scotsman who became chamber composer to George III and worked for the publisher of the early copies of the anthem. The year 1745 is the earliest date assignable to the anthem as we know it, evolved out of earlier forms. It was sung at Drury Lane to Arne's arrangement and at Covent Garden to Charles Burney's, followed by other theatres, during the Jacobite rebellion, rather as a prayer than an anthem.

NORFOLK, DUKE OF. Earl Marshal of England and premier Duke in the English peerage. As Earl Marshal he is responsible for the arrangement of the great State ceremonies and pageants. (*See* EARL MARSHAL.)

O

OATH, THE, at the Coronation service is a solemn pledge by the Sovereign to the people to observe the laws and customs of the realm as established by her predecessors. The oath was embodied in an Act of Parliament following the revolution of 1688 when James II was deposed and the Crown was conferred on William and Mary. The following was the manner of the administration of the oath at the last Coronation service:

> The Archbishop approached the King, and standing before him, administered the Coronation Oath, first asking the King, "Sir, is Your Majesty willing to take the Oath?" and the King answering, "I am willing."
>
> The Archbishop ministered these questions; and the King, having a book in his hands, answered each Question severally as follows:
>
> ARCHBISHOP: "Will you solemnly promise and swear to govern the Peoples of Great Britain, Ireland, Canada, Australia, New Zealand and the Union of South Africa, of your Possessions and the other Territories to any of them belonging or pertaining, and of your Empire of India, according to their respective Laws and Customs?"
>
> THE KING: "I solemnly promise so to do."
>
> ARCHBISHOP: "Will you to your power cause Law and Justice, in mercy, to be executed in all your Judgments?"
>
> THE KING: "I will."
>
> ARCHBISHOP: "Will you to the utmost of your power maintain the Laws of God, the true Profession of the Gospel? Will you to the utmost of your power maintain in the United Kingdom the Protes-

tant Reformed Religion established by Law? And will you maintain and preserve inviolably the Settlement of the Church of England, and the Doctrine, Worship, Discipline, and Government thereof, as by Law established in England? And will you preserve unto the Bishops and Clergy of England, and to the Churches therein committed to their charge, all such Rights and Privileges, as by Law do or shall appertain to them, or any of them?"

THE KING: "All this I promise to do."

Then the King, arising out of his Chair, supported as before, and assisted by the Lord Great Chamberlain, the Sword of State being carried before him, went to the Altar, and there being uncovered, made his Solemn Oath in the sight of all the People, to observe the Promises: Laying his Right hand upon the Holy Gospel in the Great Bible, which was now brought from the Altar by the Archbishop, and tendered to him as he knelt upon the steps, saying these words:

Coronation Roll

"The things which I have here before promised, I will perform and keep. So help me God."

Then the King kissed the Book, and signed the Oath.

At one time the sovereign took the oath upon the four Gospels, and at the British Museum is the Latin version of the Gospels used for King Athelstan at his crowning at Kingston-on-Thames in the year 925. It was thereafter used, at least, until the reign of Charles I.

The Queen is required to sign her name at the foot of the oath inscribed on a piece of vellum attached to the Coronation Roll—the complete official record of the ceremonies, which is afterwards preserved in the Records of the Court of Chancery. When George IV was crowned in 1821 the vellum with a copy of the oath was by some mischance absent from the altar. It appeared that the proceedings must be delayed while the missing document was traced; but the King's presence of mind was equal to the occasion. At his own suggestion he inscribed his signature to the oath in one of the printed copies of the Order of Service, a fact which was testified to by the Archbishop in a memorandum added to the Roll.

OBLATION, or OFFERING, is made by the newly crowned Sovereign during the Communion service. It consists of a pall or altar-cloth and an ingot of gold of a pound weight. The pall is delivered by the Groom of the Robes to the Lord Great Chamberlain, and he, kneeling, presents it to Her Majesty; the golden ingot is handed to the Lord Great Chamberlain by the Treasurer of the Household. The Queen's offerings are received by the Archbishop of Canterbury.

The Orb

OIL. The oil used for the anointing of the Sovereign at the Coronation consists chiefly of olive oil and balm. It is believed that two vessels were used previous to the Commonwealth—one for the oil and the other for the chrism. James II is said to have paid £200 for the oil used at his Coronation. There is a legend that the Virgin Mary delivered to Thomas à Becket a stone phial containing holy oil which was placed in the ampulla and used thereafter to anoint the kings of England.

ORB, or MOUND. An emblem of sovereign power which is placed in the Queen's hand at her Coronation by the Archbishop of Canterbury, who says:

> "Receive this Imperial Robe, and Orb; and the Lord your God endure you with knowledge and wisdom, with majesty and with power from on high; the Lord embrace you with His mercy on every side; the Lord cloath you with the Robe of Righteousness, and with the garments of salvation. And when you see this Orb set under the Cross remember that the whole world is subject to the Power and Empire of Christ our Redeemer."

As token of imperial power the Orb appears to have originated amongst the Romans. It was adopted as a token in general use by our Saxon kings, although it was not included in the coronation ceremonial of the investiture until a much later date.

There is some uncertainty when the Orb first was introduced at the coronation. One historian of the Regalia states that its introduction dates back no further than 1685, but in this he is certainly in error. Investiture with the Orb is not mentioned in the Liber Regalis of Richard II, but it was used at some of the Tudor crownings. The investiture with the Orb was omitted at the crowning of Charles I and Charles II, but was resumed at the coronation of James II and has since continued.

When the double crowning of William and Mary took place, a second Orb had to be specially made, for the Orb, being a token of supreme political power, had never been placed in the hands of a queen consort. Mary, however, as a queen regnant, had to be provided for exactly as her husband, although as her Orb was not likely to be used again it was made on a smaller scale.

The Sovereign's Orb is a golden ball, six inches in diameter. Around its circumference is a gold band, ornamented with diamonds, sapphires, rubies, and emeralds. From the band rises a golden arch, in which similar gems are set, and this is surmounted by a cross of gold, which rises from a fine amethyst. The cross, splendidly set with diamonds, has at its centre a sapphire on one side and at the other an emerald. Four large pearls are at the angles of the cross, and three more at the ends of it. The height of Orb and cross is eleven inches.

P

PATINA. This is a very handsome gold dish made for William and Mary in 1691–2 together with the Chalice. The Patina is more than twenty-four inches in diameter and the centre contains a representation of the Last Supper in high relief. Underneath this is a panel displaying the cipher of William and Mary surmounted by a royal crown. The dish has a wide rim on which are represented in high relief four winged cherubims with foliage, fruit, and garlands between.

POET LAUREATE. An office conferred by letters patent on a poet, who receives a stipend as a member of the Royal Household. At one time holders of the office were expected to compose verse for State occasions, but this duty is no longer enforced. Dryden was the first to receive the title officially.

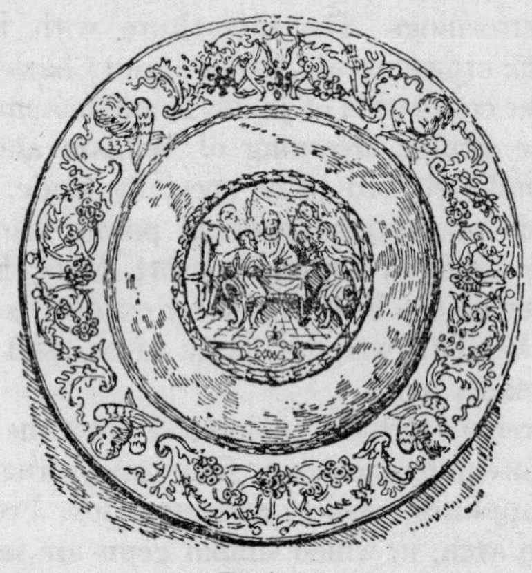

Patina

After him came Shadwell, Tate, Rowe, Eusden, Cibber, Whitehead, T. Warton, Pye, Southey, Wordsworth, Tennyson, Alfred Austin, Robert Bridges, and the present holder, John Masefield, who was appointed on May 9, 1930. Mr. Masefield was born in 1878, and as a youth went to the training-ship *Conway*. His love of ships and the sea, which finds expression in many of his best-known poems, was early inculcated, for he ran away to sea and spent his early manhood undergoing experiences which provided him with material for *Salt-Water Ballads* and other poems. On marrying in 1903 and settling down in London he began to establish himself as poet, dramatist, and novelist. On its appearance in 1911 his narrative poem *The Everlasting Mercy* created great interest. Among his novels are *Captain Margaret, Multitude and Solitude, Sard Harker*, and *Odtaa*. Mr. Masefield, who lives in Berkshire, received the Order of Merit in 1935. As Poet Laureate he has written poems on royal occasions such as the departure of King George VI for South Africa, the Queen's wedding as Princess Elizabeth, the birth of Prince Charles.

PRECEDENCE. The Order of Precedence stems from the Sovereign. Queen Elizabeth's accession accordingly brought big changes in the positions of certain members of the Royal Family. Before George VI's death the Sovereign was followed in the official Table of Precedence by his grandson, Prince Charles. Then came the Duke of Gloucester, with seniority among the Dukes of the Blood Royal, the Duke of Windsor, the Duke of Edinburgh and the King's nephew, the Duke of Kent. Other nephews followed. In his own list of precedence the King placed the Duke of Edinburgh with Princess Elizabeth.

Queen Elizabeth by Royal Warrant ordained that her husband should hold precedence next to herself. Thereafter follows Prince Charles, then the Queen's uncles, the Duke of Gloucester, and the Duke of Windsor. Her cousin, the Duke of Kent, as a Royal Duke, retains his place, but the rest of King George VI's nephews move down as cousins of the Sovereign, some by nearly 200 places. Prince William of Gloucester, as elder son of a Duke of the Blood Royal, falls back about 30 places and now ranks between the Dukes not of Blood Royal and marquesses. His brother, Prince Richard, and the Duke of Kent's brother, Prince Michael, as younger sons, go down a further 160 places, ranking after earls.

The order authorized by the Queen in prayers for the Royal Family is: The Queen, Queen Elizabeth the Queen Mother, Queen Mary, the Duke of Edinburgh, Prince Charles Duke of Cornwall, and all other members of the Royal Family.

PRIME MINISTER, or PREMIER. The leading member of the Government. The office originated over two hundred years ago, but it has only recently been recognized officially in any Act of Parliament. However, since the time of

Walpole, who is generally held to be the first Prime Minister, the powers and privileges of the office have been formulated. The holder is asked by the Sovereign to form a ministry, and he thereupon chooses his own Cabinet. He is the adviser of the Crown, the connection between the Sovereign and the Cabinet.

The present Prime Minister, Mr. Winston Churchill, who returned to 10 Downing Street for the second time after winning the General Election of October 1951, little more than three months before the new reign began, was born on November 30, 1874, in the reign of Britain's last Sovereign Queen. His birthplace was Blenheim Palace, historic home of his famous ancestor, John Churchill, Duke of Marlborough. His father was Lord Randolph Churchill, third son of the seventh Duke, and his mother was an American, Miss Jennie Jerome, of New York. The architect of victory in 1939–45, he has held more ministerial posts than any other statesmen, including two vital terms as First Lord of the Admiralty.

In 1946, King George VI conferred on him the Order of Merit. In 1949 he was awarded the Grotius Medal for his services in the cause of peace. He took particular pleasure in his appointment as Lord Warden of the Cinque Ports in 1941 at King George VI's own wish that, as a mark of appreciation for his services to the country, he should fill the oldest office associated with the defence of the realm. Mr. Churchill married in 1908 Miss Clementine Ogilvy Hozier, daughter of the late Colonel Sir Henry Hozier and the late Lady Blanche Hozier, *née* Ogilvy, daughter of the seventh Earl of Airlie. They have one son, three daughters, and eight grandchildren.

PRINCE CONSORT. No special privileges are attached by the Constitution to the consort of a reigning queen. There have been only three examples in the country's history before the Duke of Edinburgh. Philip of Spain (Philip II), who married Mary I (1553–8), daughter of Henry VIII and Katharine of Aragon, was excluded from anything more than a nominal dignity, although designated King Consort. In disgust he left England after a year. Prince George of Denmark, the second example, was Queen Anne's husband, and beyond that history has recorded little about him.

Queen Victoria's husband was known for seventeen years simply as Prince Albert before he received the title of Prince Consort by individual creation. He married Queen Victoria in 1840, being granted the style His Royal Highness. In 1842 he was given the status of Consort, but it was 1857 before he was created Prince Consort. He died four years later in 1861.

The Duke of Edinburgh, Consort of Queen Elizabeth, abandoned his foreign rank and title as H.R.H. Prince Philip of Greece when he became a British subject in February 1947. It was as Lieut. Philip Mountbatten, R.N., that he became engaged to Princess Elizabeth in July the same year. On the eve of their wedding the following November King George VI created him Prince Philip, Duke of Edinburgh, Earl of Merioneth, Baron Greenwich and Knight of the Garter.

PRINCE OF WALES, title conferred by the Sovereign on the heir apparent to the throne. (*See* WALES, PRINCE OF.)

PRINCESS ROYAL. This title belongs as of right to the eldest daughter of the Sovereign, but there cannot be two Princesses Royal at the same time. Princess Mary, only daughter of King George V, and aunt of Queen Elizabeth, was declared Princess Royal following the death of the previous holder of this title, the Dowager Duchess of Fife, eldest daughter of King Edward VII, who died January 4, 1931. (*See under* ROYAL FAMILY.)

PRIVY PURSE, KEEPER OF THE. The money fixed in the Civil List for the private and personal use of the monarch is termed the Privy Purse, and the Keeper is the official charged with payments of all private expenses of the Sovereign. Lord Tryon, who succeeded Sir Ulick Alexander in October 1952, had served as Deputy Keeper for three years. Commander Sir Dudley Colles is Deputy Keeper and Deputy Treasurer to Her Majesty.

Q

QUEEN MOTHER, QUEEN ELIZABETH, widow of King George VI. (*See under* ROYAL FAMILY.)

QUEEN'S CHAMPION. (*See* KING'S CHAMPION.)

QUEENS REGNANT. There have been five Sovereign Queens of England before the accession of Elizabeth II. They were:

Mary I .	1553–1558
Elizabeth I	1558–1603
Mary II .	1689–1694
Anne .	1702–1714
Victoria .	1837–1901

Mary I, daughter of Henry VIII and Katharine of Aragon, married Philip of Spain (Philip II). Although her husband was designated King Consort and the statutes were enacted under the joint names of Philip and Mary, he was excluded from anything more than a nominal dignity and after a year left England in disgust as a result. The great Queen Elizabeth I, Henry VIII's daughter by Anne Boleyn, never married. Mary II, eldest daughter of James II, shared the Throne equally with her husband, William of Orange, William III. They were proclaimed King and Queen and after her death he reigned alone for eight years. Anne, her sister, had as consort Prince George of Denmark. Victoria married Prince Albert of Saxe-Coburg-Gotha in 1840. Two years later his status was established as that of consort and after seventeen years of marriage, in 1857 he was created Prince Consort. He died four years later.

R

RECOGNITION. The Recognition, or presentation of the Sovereign to the assembled congregation, is the first principal ceremony of the Coronation service. Having entered

Westminster Abbey by the Great West Door, the Sovereign marches in procession up the nave and mounts the theatre, or platform, erected in the centre of the Abbey. As Her Majesty stands in the centre of the theatre, the Archbishop of Canterbury says in a clear voice:

> "Sirs, I here present unto you Queen Elizabeth, your undoubted Queen; Wherefore all you who are come this day to do your homage and service, are you willing to do the same?"

It is a solemn invitation to the congregation to declare their acceptance of the new Sovereign, and after its initial delivery it is repeated once at each of the three remaining sides of the platform, around which the Archbishop proceeds, attended by a procession of the high officials of State. The Queen turns herself as the procession moves round, so that she may face that section of the congregation which the Primate is addressing. At the end of each invitation the assembly raise a great shout of acclamation, thereby testifying their willingness to do their homage, service, and bounden duty to the Queen whom they recognize. In the oldest coronation rituals the ceremony now termed Recognition was styled "election", although even in the Anglo-Saxon kingdom the election was carried out by the Witan previous to the crowning itself. "Recognition" is a feudal term for the acknowledgment by a vassal of the succession of a landed heir.

When William the Conqueror was crowned, the Recognition ceremony was the cause of a riot. King William was still an enemy amongst enemies at the time of his coronation at Christmas in the year 1066, and his troops had been warned to be in readiness for any disturbance. Saxons and Normans formed the congregation in the Abbey, and as neither spoke the other's language the service was conducted in Saxon and Norman by the Archbishop of York and the Bishop of Coutances. When the question of the Recognition was put to the congregation a babel of sound arose, instead of a unanimous note of acclamation—the result not of any Saxon opposition, but of the mingling of the two languages. This was apparent within the Abbey. But troops on guard outside mistook the discordant sounds for evidence of Saxon discord, and began to take strenuous action against the Saxon crowds gathered around. The hubbub outside excited the congregation within. In the *mêlée*, some buildings were set on fire, and very soon the entire congregation hurried out of the Abbey, first to investigate, and then to join in the fracas. The crowning of the Conqueror was completed with scarcely an onlooker to witness it, except those whose duty required them to remain to take part in the ceremonies.

REGALIA. A term derived from the Latin word for King, and applied to the articles associated with the office of King, otherwise called the Crown Jewels. They consist of crowns and sceptres, orbs, swords, maces, and the like. They are kept in the Wakefield Tower at the Tower of London, where thousands of people see them every year. The principal objects in the Regalia are taken to Westminster Abbey for use in the Coronation. Descriptions of the principal objects in the collection are to be found under their various names:

CROWNS	SWORDS
SCEPTRES	SPURS
ORBS	RINGS
AMPULLA	BRACELETS

Most of the objects in the Regalia are less than three hundred years old, for the old Crown Jewels, including the ancient Crown of England, which was probably worn by King Alfred the Great, were destroyed after King Charles I had been executed at the time of the Commonwealth. They were melted down and the gold was sold for what it would fetch. After the Restoration, King Charles II gave orders for the making of a new Regalia on the model of the old. Various additions have been made since his time, including the two wonderful objects, the Crown of India and Queen Mary's Crown.

In olden days the Crown Jewels were kept at Westminster Abbey in a strong-room known as the Chapel of the Pyx. During the reign of Edward I, however, the place was broken into by monks, and some of the jewels, and much of the King's treasure, stolen. As a consequence, the Crown Jewels were ordered to be removed from the Abbey and to be placed at the Tower of London for greater security. Even here, however, a daring attempt was made to steal them in the reign of Charles II by Colonel Blood, who posed as a parson, with two associates. They overpowered the man in charge of the Jewel House and knocked him senseless, and began to pocket the gems. By chance the alarm was raised and Blood and his gang had to make off with only a portion of their intended booty. They got clear of the Tower, and, mounting the horses waiting for them, began to ride off. They were overtaken, however, and the major portion of the jewels was saved. Blood was pardoned by King Charles, and became quite a figure at Court. There was another attempt at robbery in 1815, when a woman forced her hand through the iron bars, seized the Crown, and attempted to pull it through, and committed some injury. In 1842 a fire broke out, and, but for the courage of those in charge, the whole collection would probably have perished. Following this, the Regalia was transferred to the Wakefield Tower, where it has been housed to the present day, except that for greater safety from bombs and air raids it was transferred to Windsor Castle during the two World Wars. During the last war a V-bomb damaged a wall of the Jewel House at the Tower.

REGENCY. If the Sovereign were incapacitated for reasons of ill-health, or any other cause, from discharging the royal duties, a Regent would be appointed to undertake these functions. The Government early in 1937 brought in a Bill to make provision for the appointment of a Regent. It provided that a Regent would discharge the royal function should the Sovereign be incapacitated by reason of infirmity of mind or body, or be under the age of eighteen years. The Regent would be the person next in line of succession to the Crown and not disqualified or under twenty-one years of age. At the time the Act was passed the Duke of Gloucester would have been the Regent. Now it would be Princess Margaret. If the Sovereign were absent abroad, or were suffering from a minor illness, a

Regent would not be needed, but instead a Council of State would carry out the royal functions.

RINGS. The Sovereign's Ring which is called the Wedding Ring of England is placed upon the fourth finger of the Queen's right hand during her Coronation. It is the symbol of the union of the Queen with her people. As he places it on the Sovereign's finger, the Primate says:

> "Receive this Ring, the ensign of kingly dignity, and of defence of the Catholic Faith; and as you are this day solemnly invested in the government of an earthly kingdom, so may you be sealed

Sovereign's Ring

Queen Consort's Ring

Queen Victoria's Ring

> with that Spirit of promise which is the earnest of an heavenly inheritance, and reign with Him who is the blessed and only Potentate, to whom be glory for ever and ever. Amen."

The Ring is adorned with a ruby set by Richard II. Charles I added a setting of diamonds, and William IV a sapphire. Also in the Regalia is Queen Victoria's Coronation ring, given to her by her uncle and predecessor, William IV. The central stone in this ring is a large ruby set in diamonds. Tradition states that the more closely the ring fits the finger of the Sovereign the longer will the reign last, and the more beloved by the people will the monarch be. Queen Victoria's ring was made for her little finger, but the Archbishop at her Coronation forced it upon the wedding finger, which caused the Queen very much discomfort, and great difficulty was experienced in removing the ring when the ceremony was ended. Mary II, joint ruler of England with her Dutch husband William of Orange, had her engagement ring enlarged for use at the Coronation. The Queen was much perturbed because by some mischance her ring was placed upon her husband's

The Royal Arms

finger instead of her own, which was considered to be a bad omen. The Queen Consort's ring is a small replica of the Sovereign's ring.

ROD OF EQUITY. Otherwise the Sceptre with the Dove, which is placed in the left hand of the Sovereign at the Coronation by the Archbishop, who says, "Receive the Rod of equity and mercy: and God . . . assist you in the administration and exercise of all those powers which He hath given you. . . ." The dove is symbolical of the Holy Ghost, Who is considered to control the actions of monarchs. This Sceptre, three feet six inches long, and made of gold, is surmounted with a cross on which stands a dove with outstretched wings, made of white enamel with golden feet, eyes, and beak. It was made for the coronation of Charles II.

ROYAL ARMS. From Queen Victoria's accession the Royal Arms have been a combination of the insignia of England, Scotland, and Ireland—the three lions of England, the Scottish red lion rampant, and the Irish harp, the whole encircled with the Garter. James I introduced the unicorn from the Scottish Royal Arms as a royal supporter sinister in place of Elizabeth I's dragon rampant, the crowned lion dexter remaining, as it still does. The motto, *Dieu et mon droit,* was adopted by Richard I after he used it as the watchword in his victory over the French at Gisors. The crest is the Imperial Crown on a royal helmet, surmounted by a crowned lion.

ROYAL COMPANY OF ARCHERS. Body Guard of the Queen for Scotland. The Captain-General of the Royal Company of Archers, Lord Elphinstone, K.T., an uncle of the Queen by marriage, is Gold Stick for Scotland at the Coronation. (*See also* GOLD STICKS.)

ROYAL FAMILY—THE HOUSE OF WINDSOR

QUEEN ELIZABETH II, the sixth Queen Regnant and the forty-first Sovereign since the Norman Conquest, acceded to the Throne at the age of twenty-five, in circumstances unique in history. Her father, King George VI, died at Sandringham in his sleep in the early hours of February 6, 1952. The night that Princess Elizabeth became Queen without knowing it she was in Kenya, dressed in brown slacks and a bush-jacket, spending the night observing jungle animals from the Treetops Hotel in a giant fig tree overlooking a waterhole in the Aberdare Forest game reserve. Her Majesty and the Duke of Edinburgh had been photographing big game at the waterhole while staying at Sagana Lodge, Kenya's wedding gift to the royal couple.

The Queen was born on April 21, 1926, at 17 Bruton Street, Mayfair, the London residence of her mother's parents, the

Earl and Countess of Strathmore. At that time her father and mother were the Duke and Duchess of York. She was christened, in the private chapel at Buckingham Palace by the Archbishop of Canterbury, Elizabeth Alexandra Mary, the names of her mother, great-grandmother, and grandmother. From her earliest years her golden hair and bright blue eyes captivated the people of the country and Commonwealth.

Her childhood was spent mainly at 145 Piccadilly, her father's town home until his accession. The house, like her birthplace, was demolished by a German bomb. Gradually the little girl came to realize the significance of her royal destiny. She was a bridesmaid at the weddings of her uncles, the late Duke of Kent and the Duke of Gloucester, watched the funeral procession of her grandfather, King George V, and dropped a curtsey as the coffin passed her home. The Princess was in the schoolroom at 145 Piccadilly when she was told that, following the abdication of her uncle, her father and mother had become King and Queen. She went on with her lessons.

Queen's Private Cipher

She became a Girl Guide as a member of the Buckingham Palace troop. During the war she stayed at Windsor Castle, the King having decided that his daughters should remain in Britain to share the dangers and anxieties of the people. She next joined the Sea Rangers. In 1940, when fourteen, she performed her first public duty by broadcasting to the children of the Empire. On her sixteenth birthday His Majesty appointed her Honorary Colonel of the Grenadier Guards. When she reached calling-up age of eighteen the Princess insisted on joining the A.T.S., underwent an N.C.O.'s course at an Aldershot training centre, and rose to the rank of Junior Commander. In July 1944 she served for the first time as a Counsellor of State during the King's visit to the

Mediterranean theatre of war. At Clydebank in November the same year she launched the battleship *Vanguard*, which was to take her, her parents, and her sister, Princess Margaret, to South Africa little more than two years later.

In the meantime the news began to spread of a royal romance in the making, and pictures of Prince Philip of Greece, a lieutenant in His Majesty's Navy, appeared in the newspapers. The Royal Family sailed from Portsmouth for South Africa on a 23,000-mile tour on January 31, 1947. Princess Elizabeth celebrated her twenty-first birthday in the Union and in a broadcast on that day from Government House, Cape Town, dedicated herself to her imperial destiny.

On July 9, 1947, two months after the Royal Family's return home, the announcement was made:

> "It is with the greatest pleasure that the King and Queen announce the betrothal of their dearly beloved daughter to Lieut. Philip Mountbatten, R.N., son of the late Prince Andrew of Greece and Princess Andrew (Princess Alice of Battenberg), to which union the King has gladly given his consent."

This was the name that Prince Philip had taken when he became a naturalized British subject the previous February. In 1944 he had renounced his right of succession to the throne of the Hellenes. Not quite five years older than the Princess, he was, like her, a great-great grandchild of Queen Victoria. The wedding took place at Westminster Abbey on November 20, 1947, the Archbishop of Canterbury, Dr. Fisher, officiating. Vast crowds lined the streets. The procession scenes were televised, while millions of people the world over heard the ceremony broadcast. On the eve of the wedding Lieut. Mountbatten was created Duke of Edinburgh, Earl of Merioneth, Baron Greenwich, and Knight of the Garter, and granted the style of His Royal Highness. The Princess's allowance of £15,000 a year, received since her twenty-first birthday, was increased to £40,000. The Duke was granted £10,000 a year. Great satisfaction was caused throughout the Commonwealth when a son, Prince Charles, was born to them at Buckingham Palace on November 14, 1948. Thousands gathered outside the palace till well into the night.

In July 1949 the Princess and the Duke took up residence at Clarence House, their London home until Easter 1952, for the modernization of which Parliament had voted £50,000. They had previously divided their time between Buckingham Palace and Windlesham Moor, Sunningdale.

With her husband, Princess Elizabeth undertook an onerous programme of public duties, increased by the King's ill-health. When the Duke resumed his naval career and served with the Mediterranean Fleet, the Princess flew to Malta to be with him on several occasions, in 1949, 1950, and 1951. They celebrated the second anniversary of their wedding there. In the summer of 1950 the Duke flew home to be present at the birth of their second child, Princess Anne, at Clarence House on August 15.

Of all her many popular public appearances as Princess Elizabeth, Her Majesty's greatest personal triumph was when, in the tunic of the Grenadier Guards and wearing an attractive tricorne hat, she rode to Horse Guards Parade to take the salute at the Trooping the Colour in the King's absence on His Majesty's official birthday in 1951. She repeated this success in the Scots Guards tunic last June and on that occasion it was the first time in the history of these islands that a reigning Queen took part. In October the same year came the coast-to-coast tour of Canada in which the royal couple covered 16,500 miles and also visited Washington as guests of President Truman. Both in the Dominion and in the United States they scored a personal success and made a deep impression, the Princess with her grace and beauty, the Duke with his easy informality.

Sharing the royal interest in racing, the Princess had her first win in her own colours at Hurst Park in 1950 with Astrakhan, a wedding present from the Aga Khan. She also owned the steeplechaser Monaveen, in partnership with her mother. Her yacht *Bluebottle*, presented by the Island Sailing Club at Cowes, took part in several regattas and the Princess became the only lady member of the Royal Yacht Squadron in 1947 when the Duke became a full member.

After the Canadian tour came the decision that the Heiress

Presumptive to the Throne, with her husband, should undertake the projected tour of Australia and New Zealand instead of the King and Queen in view of King George VI's state of health. They left London on January 31, 1952, by air, and arrived at Nairobi, Kenya, on February 1. Then came the sudden news of the King's death five days later. At once the new Queen decided to fly home. She was delayed by storms, but arrived next day and was publicly proclaimed Queen and made her accession declaration at St. James's Palace on February 8. It was 115 years since a Queen of England had been proclaimed and 51 years since a Sovereign Queen had sat on the throne. The sixth Queen Regnant in our history came to the Throne at the same age, twenty-five, as her great namesake, the first Queen Elizabeth. The day after she ascended the Throne, the Prime Minister Mr. Churchill, in a moving and magnificent broadcast on the death of King George VI, closed with this characteristic passage:

> "Famous have been the reigns of our Queens. Some of the greatest periods of our history have unfolded under their sceptre. Now that we have the second Queen Elizabeth also ascending the Throne in her 26th year, our thoughts are carried back nearly 400 years to the magnificent figure who presided over, and in many ways embodied and inspired, the grandeur and genius of the Elizabethan age. Queen Elizabeth II, like her predecessor, did not pass her childhood in any certain expectation of the Crown. But already we know her well and we understand why her gifts and those of her husband, the Duke of Edinburgh, have stirred the parts of our Commonwealth she has been able to visit. I, whose youth was passed in the august, unchallenged and tranquil glories of the Victorian era, may well feel a thrill in invoking once more the prayer and the anthem, 'God Save the Queen!' "

DUKE OF EDINBURGH. His Royal Highness Prince Philip, Duke of Edinburgh, like the Queen, is a great-great grandchild of Queen Victoria. His father, who died in 1944, was Prince Andrew of Greece and Denmark, who married Princess Alice of Battenberg, sister of Earl Mountbatten of Burma. Popular, handsome, and an easy mixer, Prince Philip had a fine war record in the Navy and is known as a sportsman on the cricket and polo fields and in his favourite pastime of sailing. Born on June 10, 1923, he was sent to a preparatory school at Cheam.

Then at the age of thirteen he went to the school in Baden of Kurt Hahn, who was soon exiled by the Nazis. Hahn became a British subject and established his school at Gordonstoun, in Morayshire, in the north-east of Scotland, and Philip proceeded there. An all-round sportsman, he captained the school in cricket and hockey and took up small-boat sailing with enthusiasm.

He and Princess Elizabeth met many times as small children. Both were often at the Park Lane home of his uncle, then Lord Louis Mountbatten, and Philip was a schoolboy guest at her father's Coronation. While he was at Dartmouth Naval College the King, Queen, and the two Princesses visited it and the young couple met again. After winning the King's Dirk as the best cadet of his term, Philip was commissioned as midshipman in 1940 and joined the *Ramillies* with the Mediterranean Fleet. At the Battle of Matapan in 1941 he was in charge of a section of searchlight control. Promoted Sub-Lieutenant next year, he was present in the destroyer *Wallace* at the Canadian landings in Sicily before appointment as First Lieutenant in H.M.S. *Whelp*, a new destroyer, in 1944. This vessel joined the Pacific Fleet, and at the surrender of the Japanese Fleet in Tokyo Bay in 1945 Philip met his uncle, then Supreme Commander South-East Asia.

During his active war service he kept up correspondence with the Princess and spent several leaves at Windsor Castle. At Christmas 1943 he watched her production of *Aladdin* there. As early as 1945 their names were linked in Court circles. In 1946 Philip was a guest at Balmoral and was generally believed to have asked for her hand. The King advised them, "Wait and see how you feel in another six months." The following February Philip, who had renounced his right of succession to the throne of the Hellenes in 1944, became a British subject. Soon after the Royal Family's return from their South African tour in 1947 the King announced in July the betrothal of his elder daughter to Lieut. Philip Mountbatten, R.N.

A son was born, Prince Charles, second in line of succession to the Throne, at Buckingham Palace on November 14, 1948, a year after the Abbey ceremony. Marriage and the consequent assumption of a share of the Princess's royal duties did not at once end the Duke's naval career, in which he attained the rank of Lieutenant Commander. In 1949 he was appointed First Lieutenant of H.M.S. *Chequers*, leader of the First Destroyer Flotilla, Mediterranean Fleet. His wife flew to join him in Malta and they celebrated the second anniversary of their wedding there. In the summer of 1950 the Duke flew back to England for the birth of their second child, Princess Anne, at Clarence House on August 15. Once more in Malta in September, he took over his first command, the frigate *Magpie*. The Princess again joined him in 1951 and they visited Italy, being received by the Pope.

On his return to Britain the Duke enhanced his prestige by a thoughtful speech as President of the British Association to the Empire's scientists assembled in Edinburgh. A success of another kind was a win at Cowes in his yacht *Cowslip*, presented to him by the people of Cowes.

PRINCE CHARLES, DUKE OF CORNWALL, was born at Buckingham Palace on November 14, 1948. When a little over three years of age he became Heir Apparent on the death of his grandfather, King George VI, on February 6, 1952. He was the King's first grandchild and Queen Mary's first great-grandchild.

He was born a prince owing to King George VI's amendment by letters patent, issued five days before Prince Charles's birth and dated October 22, 1948, of George V's rules laid down in July 1917, when the Royal Family adopted the name of Windsor. By George V's rules only grandchildren of the Sovereign in the male line were entitled to the style of Royal Highness and Prince or Princess. George VI amended these rules so that the royal style would extend also to children of his elder daughter, the Heiress Presumptive to the Throne, Princess Elizabeth. The amendment did not apply to any children of Princess Margaret.

The Prince was christened Charles Philip Arthur George by the Archbishop of Canterbury, Dr. Fisher, in the music-room at Buckingham Palace on December 15, 1948. The private chapel there was still unsuitable through being damaged by a bomb during the war. The infant was dressed in the historic Honiton lace robe made for Queen Victoria and used at the christening of all her children and most members of the Royal Family since then, including the present Queen and Prince Charles's sister, Princess Anne.

Sponsors at the christening were King George VI, Queen Mary, Princess Margaret, the Dowager Marchioness of Milford Haven, paternal great-grandmother, Lady Brabourne, his first cousin once removed and elder daughter of Earl Mountbatten of Burma, the Hon. David Bowes-Lyon, maternal great-uncle and, by proxy, King Haakon of Norway, great-great uncle, and Prince George of Greece, great-great uncle on his father's side.

Under charter of Edward III in 1337, Prince Charles, on becoming Heir Apparent on the accession of his mother, automatically became Duke of Cornwall and entitled to the revenues of the Duchy of Cornwall. These were estimated in 1937 at £108,000 a year. He also assumed the Scottish titles of the Heir Apparent, which came through James I: Duke of Rothesay, Earl of Carrick, Baron of Renfrew, Lord of the Isles, and Prince and Great Steward of Scotland.

PRINCESS ANNE. Second child of the Queen and the Duke of Edinburgh, was born at Clarence House on August 15, 1950. She was christened in the music-room at Buckingham Palace on October 23 by the Archbishop of York, Dr. Garbett. She was given the names Anne Elizabeth Alice Louise.

QUEEN ELIZABETH THE QUEEN MOTHER, widow of King George VI, whom see, was the first subject for nearly three hundred years to occupy the Consort's Throne. Though not of royal birth, she is of royal descent, tracing her ancestry back to King Robert the Bruce and the old Stuart dynasty. She was the first Scotswoman to be a Queen of England since Matilda, first consort of Henry I and daughter of King Malcolm; born 1079, married 1100, died 1118.

The Queen Mother was Lady Elizabeth Angela Marguerite Bowes-Lyon, youngest but one of the ten children of the fourteenth Earl and the Countess of Strathmore. This is an ancient and illustrious Scottish family on whom the Barony of Glamis, Macbeth's Glamis, was conferred in 1445, the

Earldom of Strathmore in 1606, and the Earldom of Strathmore and Kinghorne in 1677. Lady Elizabeth was born on August 4, 1900, at her parents' Hertfordshire home, St. Paul's Waldenbury, where, when she was twenty-two, the Duke of York was to propose to her.

When she was five she met Prince Albert, aged ten, King George V's second son, at a children's party. She was later chosen as a playmate for Princess Mary. During the First World War when Glamis Castle, her family's ancestral home, where Princess Margaret was born, was converted into a hospital, Lady Elizabeth helped in caring for the wounded. After the Armistice she again met Prince Albert, the childhood acquaintanceship ripened, and in 1921 the King's son, by then Duke of York, was invited to Glamis. In the next year Lady Elizabeth was one of Princess Mary's bridesmaids. Then in January 1923 her engagement to the Duke was announced.

Their marriage, in Westminster Abbey in April of that year, proved a happy partnership of devoted family life and public service. The smiling Duchess developed into a national figure and became the radiant Queen and helpmate of the King in the sixteen testing years of his reign. During his illness she carried on with dauntless serenity, deputizing for His Majesty in maintaining the Royal Family's tradition of service to the nation.

PRINCESS MARGARET, sister of the Queen, was born on August 21, 1930, at Glamis Castle, the Queen Mother's ancestral home. She was the first royal infant to be born in Scotland since Charles I at Dunfermline in 1600. The Princess was given the names Margaret, associated for centuries with Scottish queens, and Rose after her mother's sister, Countess Granville. During the war Princess Margaret headed "The Margarets Fund", to which Margarets throughout the Empire contributed to help Y.M.C.A. work for the Forces. With her sister she organized and took part in concerts for war charities and the first royal pantomime in December 1941 in aid of the Royal Household Wool Fund. As Cinderella Princess Margaret scored a success and revealed a talent for mimicry. Pantomimes after that became a regular feature of wartime life at Windsor Castle. Her first unaccompanied public engagement was the launching of the liner *Edinburgh Castle* in 1947 at Belfast. She celebrated her official coming of age—her eighteenth birthday—at Balmoral and was presented with her personal Standard.

QUEEN MARY, grandmother of Her Majesty, born at Kensington Palace, May 26, 1867. Queen Mary's mother, born 1833, was Princess Mary Adelaide, youngest daughter of the Duke of Cambridge, son of George III. Within a month of first meeting Francis Duke of Teck, only son of the Duke Alexander of Wurttemberg, she married him in June 1866. Princess May, as she was called, was the only daughter and eldest child of the marriage, and she was brought up at White Lodge, Richmond. She was engaged to the Duke of Clarence, elder son of King Edward VII and Queen Alexandra, but he died before their marriage. Princess May's marriage to the Duke of York, second son of King Edward, who later became King George V, took place in July 1893. Her only surviving brother is now known as the EARL OF ATHLONE (the Queen's great-uncle); this peerage was created in 1917, when he relinquished the title of Prince Alexander of Teck. He was born in April 1874, and married in 1904 Princess Alice of Albany, now known as PRINCESS ALICE, COUNTESS OF ATHLONE. She was the only daughter of Prince Leopold, Duke of Albany, son of Queen Victoria, who married in 1882 Princess Helena of Waldeck and Pyrmont. There is one surviving child of this marriage, LADY MAY ABEL SMITH, who married in 1931.

Queen Mary's elder brother, the Marquess of Cambridge, who died in 1927, married in 1894 Lady Margaret Grosvenor, daughter of the first Duke of Westminster. Their surviving children, great-cousins of the Queen, are:

The MARQUESS OF CAMBRIDGE, born 1895, married 1923 Miss Dorothy Hastings, daughter of the Hon. Osmond Hastings, son of the thirteenth Earl of Huntingdon.

Lady Victoria Constance Mary, now the DUCHESS OF BEAUFORT, who married in 1923 the Marquess of Worcester, who became Duke of Beaufort in 1925.

Lady Helena Frances Augusta, now LADY HELENA GIBBS, who married in 1919 Colonel John Evelyn Gibbs.

UNCLES AND AUNT

1. The DUKE OF WINDSOR, born June 23, 1894, at White Lodge, Richmond Park; created Prince of Wales June 23, 1910, and invested at Caernarvon Castle, July 13, 1911; succeeded his father, George V, on January 21, 1936, as King Edward VIII; abdicated December 11, 1936. (*See* WINDSOR, DUKE OF.)

2. The PRINCESS ROYAL, Countess of Harewood, born York Cottage, Sandringham, April 25, 1897; married February 28, 1922, Viscount Lascelles, later sixth Earl of Harewood (died 1947). Two sons, cousins of the Queen:

(*i*) EARL OF HAREWOOD, born February 7, 1923; married 1949 Miss Marion Stein; one son, VISCOUNT LASCELLES, born October 21, 1950.

(*ii*) HON. GERALD LASCELLES, born August 21, 1924.

3. The DUKE OF GLOUCESTER, one of the most travelled members of the Royal Family, who would have been Regent had Princess Elizabeth acceded to the throne as a minor. Prince Henry William Frederick Albert, third son of George V and Queen Mary, was born on March 31, 1900, at York Cottage, Sandringham. He was entered at Eton as Henry Windsor, took up a military career and was created Duke of Gloucester in 1928. On November 7, 1935, he was married in the private chapel at Buckingham Palace to Lady Alice Christabel Montagu-Douglas-Scott, third daughter of the seventh Duke of Buccleuch, who shares her husband's interest in hunting, travelling, and big game shooting. In 1943 the Duke was appointed the first royal Governor-General of Australia. When he sailed the following year to take up his post his convoy was attacked off Ireland by a U-Boat, which was sunk. Two sons, cousins of the Queen:

(*i*) PRINCE WILLIAM, born December 18, 1941.

(*ii*) PRINCE RICHARD, born August 26, 1944.

COUSINS

The DUKE OF KENT, born October 9, 1935; Prince Edward George Nicholas Paul Patrick, eldest child of the first Duke of

Kent, George V's fourth son, and H.R.H. Princess Marina of Greece and Denmark; succeeded to Dukedom on August 25, 1942, when his father was killed on active service in an R.A.F. crash in the North of Scotland. Was recalled from school at Gstaad in Switzerland for his first public duty, to walk with the other Royal Dukes behind George VI's bier in the funeral procession.

PRINCESS ALEXANDRA OF KENT, born December 25, 1936, second child of the first Duke of Kent.

PRINCE MICHAEL OF KENT, born July 4, 1942, youngest child of the first Duke of Kent.

FIRST COUSINS ONCE REMOVED

PRINCESS ARTHUR OF CONNAUGHT, Duchess of Fife, daughter of the late Princess Royal, Duchess of Fife, eldest sister of George V; born May 17, 1891; married 1913 Prince Arthur of Connaught (died 1938), only son of the first Duke of Connaught, son of Queen Victoria.

PRINCE OLAV, Crown Prince of Norway, only child of the late Queen Maud of Norway, youngest sister of George V, and King Haakon; born July 2, 1903; married 1929 Princess Marthe of Sweden; one son, two daughters.

SECOND COUSIN

LORD CARNEGIE, born September 1929; nephew of Princess Arthur of Connaught and heir presumptive to Dukedom of Fife; son of the late Princess Maud of Fife, Countess of Southesk, Princess Arthur's sister, and the Earl of Southesk.

GREAT-GREAT COUSINS

LADY PATRICIA RAMSAY (Princess Victoria Patricia Helena Elizabeth of Connaught), daughter of first Duke of Connaught and grand-daughter of Queen Victoria, born March 1886; married 1919 Rear-Admiral the Hon. Sir Alexander Robert Maule Ramsay, son of the thirteenth Earl of Dalhousie.

MARQUESS OF CARISBROOKE (Alexander Albert Mountbatten), first Marquess, eldest son of Prince Henry of Battenberg and of Princess Beatrice, ninth and youngest child of Queen Victoria; born November 1886; married 1917 Lady Irene Frances Denison, daughter of second Earl of Londesborough.

H.M. VICTORIA EUGENIE, former Queen of Spain, daughter of Princess Beatrice and grand-daughter of Queen Victoria; born October 24, 1887; created Royal Highness 1906; married same year Alfonso XIII, King of Spain (resigned 1931).

ROYAL HOUSEHOLD. The Lord Chamberlain, not to be confused with the Lord Great Chamberlain (*q.v.*), is the chief officer of the Royal Household. There are also the Lord Steward and the Master of the Horse.

The TREASURER OF THE HOUSEHOLD, a political appointment, ranks next to the Lord Steward on the Board of the Green Cloth. Mr. Cedric Drewe, Conservative M.P. for Honiton, is the present holder. At the conclusion of the Coronation ceremony in the Abbey the Treasurer distributes commemorative medals. Next to this officer comes the COMPTROLLER OF THE HOUSEHOLD, who is thus the second officer under the Lord Steward. Major R. J. E. Conant, M.P. for Rutland and Stamford, holds the post, and the VICE-CHAMBERLAIN is Major H. G. Studholme, M.P. for Tavistock.

In a list of appointments to the Royal Household, published in a special *London Gazette* on July 20, 1936, it was revealed that King Edward VIII had made some important changes. He created posts of Captain of the King's Flight, and Manipulative Surgeon in the Medical Household.

The first office was filled by Flight-Lieut. (now Air Commodore) E. H. Fielden, who was King Edward VIII's personal pilot, and the first man to pilot a King of England through the air. The second office went to Sir Morton Smart, formerly medical officer in charge of the electrical department of the Hospital for Sick Children, Great Ormond Street, London. These appointments have continued since then.

Important posts in the personal service of the Sovereign are:

PRINCIPAL PRIVATE SECRETARY (since 1943) and Keeper of the Archives—Sir Alan Lascelles, born April 11, 1887.

MASTER OF THE HOUSEHOLD (since 1941)—Sir Piers Legh, born December 12, 1890.

KEEPER OF THE PRIVY PURSE—Lord Tryon.

PERMANENT LORDS IN WAITING—Earl of Cromer (since 1938), born November 29, 1877; Lord Wigram (since 1936), Private Secretary to the King, 1931–6; Keeper of the Privy Purse, 1935–6; born July 5, 1873; and the Earl of Clarendon, seventy-five, who was Lord Chamberlain from 1938 until last October.

Also on the private secretarial staff are: Major Sir Michael Adeane, born September 30, 1910 (since 1937); Lt.-Col. the Hon. Martin Charteris, born September 7, 1913 (appointed at Clarence House, 1950).

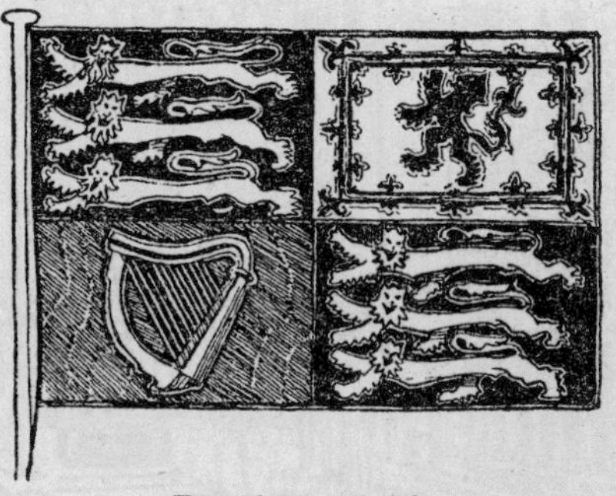

Royal Standard

The Duke of Edinburgh's Treasurer is Lt.-Gen. Sir Frederick Browning, whose wife is Daphne du Maurier, the novelist; born December 20, 1896. The General had previously been Comptroller and Treasurer to Princess Elizabeth since 1947. The Duke's Private Secretary is Lt.-Cmdr. Michael Parker, R.N. (retd.), an Australian, who was appointed equerry to Her Majesty and His Royal Highness in 1948; born June 23, 1920.

ROYAL STANDARD. The Royal Standard is the personal flag of the Sovereign and may be hoisted only when the Sovereign is present. Through many changes it came to its present form with Queen Victoria. Of its four quarterings, the first and fourth, three golden lions on a red ground, stand for England, the second, a red lion rampant on a yellow back-

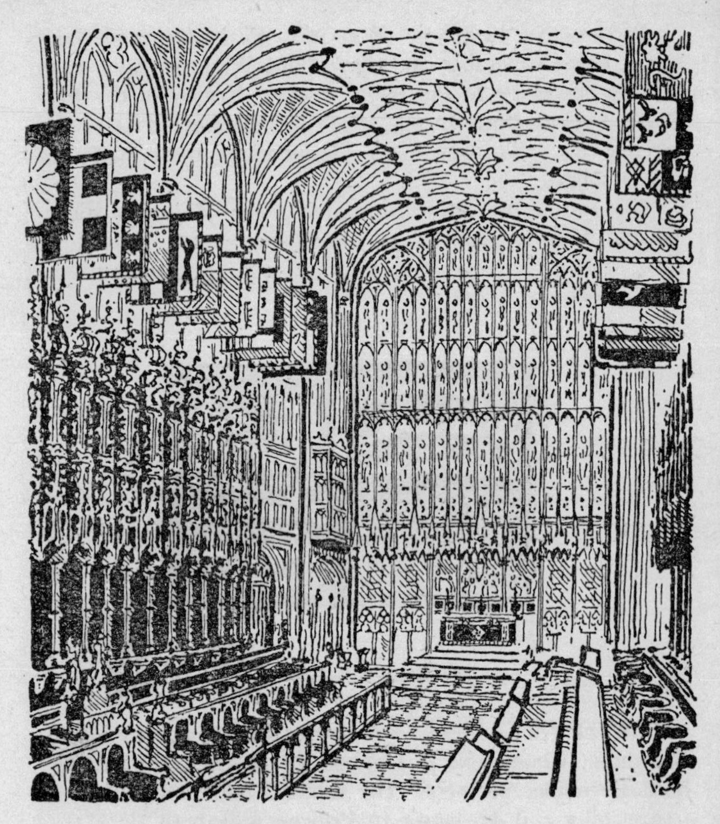

St. George's Chapel, Windsor

ground, for Scotland, and the third, a golden harp on blue, for Ireland. It is generally believed that the English lions were first used by Richard Cœur de Lion about 1195. Two of the three lions have been assigned as the arms of William the Conqueror, one each for Normandy and Maine. The accession of James VI of Scotland to the Throne of England brought the Scottish lion to the Standard and the Irish harp also took up its position.

S

ST. GEORGE'S CHAPEL, WINDSOR. Scene of the funeral service for British Sovereigns and chapel of the Order of the Garter. The original chapel by Edward III, who founded the Order in 1348, gave way to the present edifice of Edward IV, completed by Henry VII and Henry VIII. It is a masterpiece of late Perpendicular architecture. The Choir contains

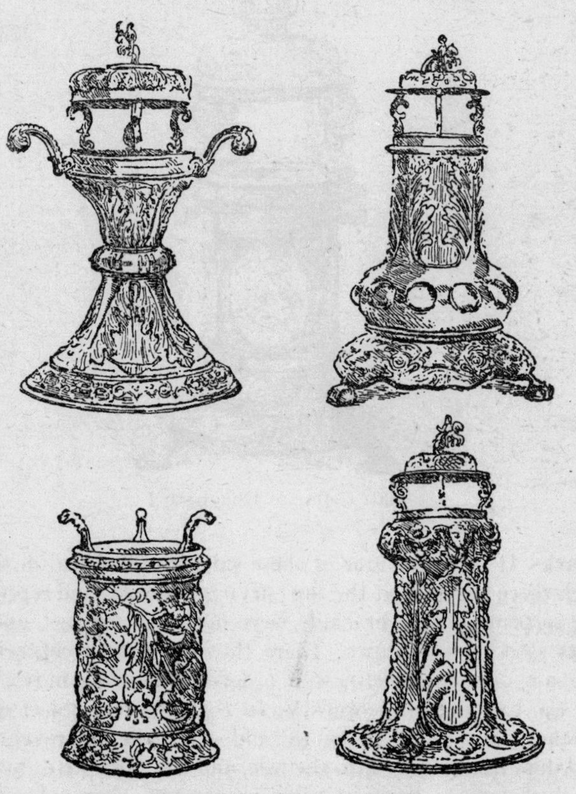

Four of St. George's Salts

the stalls of the Knights of the Garter, over which are set up the sword, helmet, crest, and banner of each knight and a plate bearing his arms and titles.

ST. GEORGE'S SALTS. There are eleven of these, of several patterns, made of gold, and dating from the time of

Salt Cellar of Elizabeth I

Charles II. A set of four of these salts is cylindrical in shape, with three brackets at the top curving outwards and representing serpents. These brackets were mistaken for legs, and the salts stood upside down. There thus being no receptacle for the salt, four small dishes were ordered to be made in readiness for the banquet of George IV. In 1918 the real object of the brackets was found to be to hold a napkin to prevent dirt and dust from falling into the salt, and the salts were inverted to their proper position after ninety-two years of misuse.

There are twelve salt-spoons of gold for use with the salt-cellars.

SALT-CELLARS. There are, in all, thirteen salt-cellars among the Regalia in the Tower. These were formerly used at the Coronation banquets, the last of which took place in

Salt of State

Westminster Hall after the Coronation of George IV. The salt-cellar of Queen Elizabeth I is the oldest piece of table plate in the Jewel House, having been handed back to the Crown after the Restoration. It is of gold, about twelve inches in height. There is a shallow receptacle for the salt, and over this is a canopy on the top of which is the figure of a knight in armour holding a two-handled sword and a shield.

The Salt of State was presented to King Charles II by the City of Exeter. It is two feet in height, of solid silver, and represents a medieval castle prepared for defence. At the four corners are turrets; cannon and guns appear from every wall. A cupola in the shape of a royal crown surmounts the walls. Costly jewels adorn the castle, and a large sapphire is placed above the portcullis. Shallow vessels to contain salt are placed under the tops of the turrets, which lift off. Little troughs to hold salt are seen under the windows.

SANDRINGHAM. The Sovereign's country house in Norfolk, with its 7000-acre estate, was bought in 1861 by

Sandringham

Edward VII when Prince of Wales. It was a favourite home of George V, who, with Queen Mary, greatly developed and improved the fine gardens. George V and George VI, both noted shots, prized the estate for its pheasant and partridge shooting. It was at Sandringham that the famous series of royal Christmas broadcasts was begun in 1932 by George V and most of them have continued to be heard all over the world from there ever since. Both George V and George VI breathed their last at Sandringham.

SAPPHIRE OF ST. EDWARD. One of the oldest gems in the Regalia. It was worn by King Edward the Confessor in his Coronation Ring. When Edward died the Ring was buried with him. In the year 1101 his shrine in Westminster Abbey was broken into and the Ring and other jewels abstracted. According to legend, the Ring was once given to St. John the Evangelist, who appeared before King Edward disguised as a pilgrim. In King Edward's time the Ring was said to possess miraculous curative power over rheumatic complaints. The stone escaped destruction during the Commonwealth. It now occupies the centre of the Cross paté surmounting the State Crown.

SCEPTRES. These stand next in importance to the Crown as emblems of kingship, and they have been used in England from the earliest times. English sceptres are of two kinds—the Sceptre with the Cross, an emblem of power and justice, and the Rod with the Dove, an emblem of equity and mercy. In all there are five sceptres among the Regalia. The most important is

The Sovereign's Royal Sceptre with Cross. This is of gold, about three feet long. The middle part is not decorated; the lower end is richly jewelled; the upper end contains the Star of Africa added by order of King Edward VII after the Cullinan diamond had been cut. Above the diamond stands a great amethyst orb with a band and an arch jewelled with rubies and diamonds. At the top of the sceptre is a cross consisting entirely of diamonds with a large emerald in the centre. This sceptre is used by the Sovereign only at the Coronation. It rests on the coffin at the funeral of the Sovereign, along with the Crown and Orb.

The Queen Consort's Sceptre with the Cross. This is of gold, two feet ten inches long, ornamented with diamonds. It was first used by Mary of Modena, wife of James II. This is surmounted by a cross with arms adorned with diamonds, standing on a golden orb with fillet and arch richly set with diamonds. The Staff is decorated with foliage composed of diamonds.

The Sovereign's Sceptre with the Dove. This is a rod of gold eight feet seven inches in length. At the top is an orb of gold with fillet and arch jewelled with diamonds. Above the orb is a golden cross on which sits a white enamelled dove with outstretched wings, and eyes, feet, and beak of gold. The dove symbolizes the Holy Ghost. Underneath the orb the sceptre is studded with a band of diamonds. The centre is ornamented with a band of enamels and gems. Near the bottom is a band of large jewels.

Two sceptres are handed to the Sovereign during the Coronation service, the Sceptre with Cross, ensign of kingly

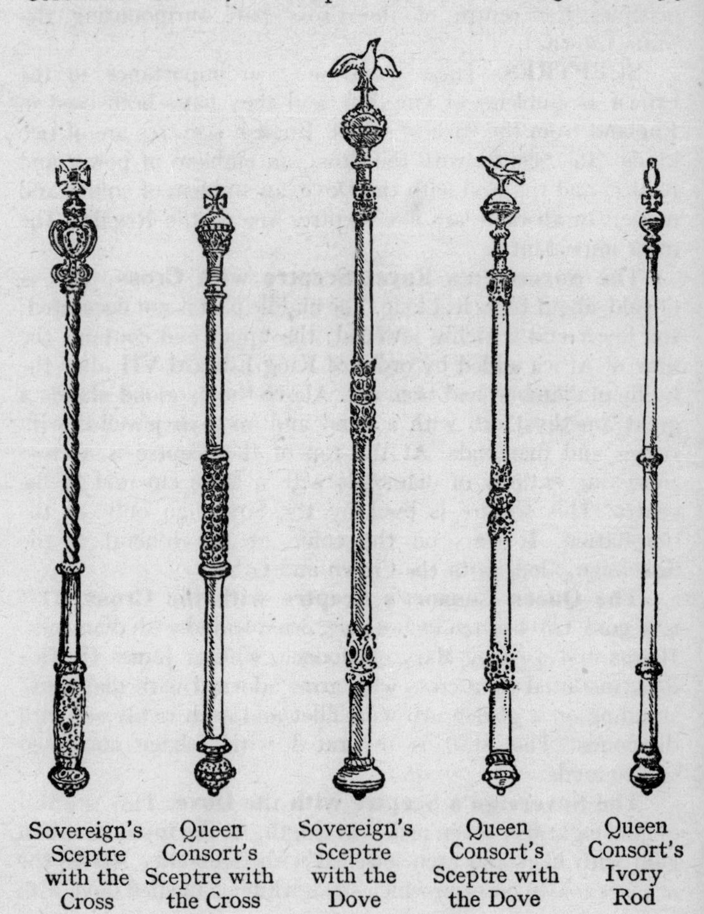

Sovereign's Sceptre with the Cross — Queen Consort's Sceptre with the Cross — Sovereign's Sceptre with the Dove — Queen Consort's Sceptre with the Dove — Queen Consort's Ivory Rod

power and justice, which the Queen holds in her right hand; and the Sceptre with Dove, token of equity and mercy, which she takes in her left hand. The Archbishop of Canterbury says:

"Receive the Rod of equity and mercy; and God, from whom all holy desires, all good counsels, and all just works do proceed, direct and assist you in the administration and exercise of all those powers which He hath given you. Be so merciful that you be not too remiss; so execute justice that you forget not mercy. Punish the wicked, protect and cherish the just, and lead your people in the way wherein they should go."

Serjeant-at-Arms, House of Commons

The Queen Consort's Sceptre with the Dove. This resembles the corresponding Sovereign's Sceptre, but it is smaller and is differently decorated; coloured gems are used in the orb with enamelling of red and white, and in the middle of the Sceptre is a band of blue enamel decorated with gems. This Sceptre was made for Mary, wife of William III. For many years it was lost, but was found in 1814 at the back of a shelf in the Jewel House.

The Queen Consort's Ivory Rod. This Rod is made of

State Coach of the Speaker of the House of Commons

three pieces of ivory with three bands of gold at the points of junction. It is three feet one and a half inches long. It has a dove at the top with closed wings, and eyes, beak, and feet of gold. The dove stands on a gold cross and this in its turn upon a gold orb. The bottom is ornamented similarly to the orb at the top. The Rod was made for Queen Mary of Modena.

SERJEANTS-AT-ARMS. At the Coronation procession within Westminster Abbey, Serjeants-at-Arms, carrying their silver-gilt maces, walk by the side of the bearers of Regalia. Of the various guards attending on the Sovereign, the Serjeants-at-Arms have the longest history. They were instituted by Richard I.

SERJEANT-AT-ARMS, HOUSE OF COMMONS. An officer who attends the Speaker, assisted by a Deputy Serjeant and an Assistant Serjeant. He sits below the bar to maintain order without the House. If a person is committed by order of the House, he apprehends him and retains him in custody. The present holder is Brigadier Sir Charles Alfred Howard, K.C.V.O., D.S.O.

SERJEANT-AT-ARMS, HOUSE OF LORDS. An office of a similar nature to the foregoing. The holder is Air Vice-Marshal Sir Paul Maltby, K.B.E., C.B., D.S.O., A.F.C.

SPEAKER OF THE HOUSE OF COMMONS. Among the Speaker's duties are those of presiding over the House of Commons, making rulings as to procedure, calling on members

Coronation Spoon

to address the House in debate, maintaining order, and signing warrants for by-election writs. The Speaker is independent of party in his official capacity and only votes if the numbers are equal—that is to say, if a casting vote is needed. When a new Parliament meets, the old Speaker, if available, is usually elected, and he holds office until a dissolution. The Speaker, who is the first commoner in the land, receives a yearly salary of £5000. The present Speaker is the Rt. Hon. William Shepherd Morrison, M.C., Q.C., who was elected to succeed Col. Clifton Brown after the 1951 General Election when for the first time since 1895 there was a contest for the post. A Scotsman, born in 1893, a Conservative M.P. since 1929, and a Minister from 1935 to 1945. Both he and his wife are barristers and they have four sons. His position entitles him to the occupancy of the Speaker's House, Palace of Westminster.

SPOON. Used during the ceremony of anointing the Sovereign. The oil contained in the golden Ampulla (*q.v.*) is poured out into the Spoon and the Archbishop dips his fingers into it and then anoints the Queen on head and hands. The Spoon is of gold and the handle is set with four pearls. It is believed to be 700 years old, and is thus the oldest article used during the Coronation ceremony. Except for the Spoon and the Ampulla, the articles of the Regalia were destroyed during the Commonwealth.

SPURS. Spurs, known as St. George's Spurs, are the symbol of knightly chivalry, and are used symbolically during the Coronation service. They were made by order of King Charles II, and are of a pattern known as "Prick"

St. George's Spurs

spurs, each spur having a sharp point in place of the usual rowels. The straps are of crimson velvet, embroidered with gold, made by order of George IV.

Formerly spurs were buckled on the heels of the Sovereign at the Coronation and at once removed, but since the time of Queen Anne this custom has been abandoned. A king's heels are now touched with the Spurs, but at Queen Victoria's Coronation they were merely presented to her. The Spurs are carried by the rightful claimant of the honour in the procession. At the Coronation of King George V, Lord Grey and the Earl of Loudoun were each ascribed the right to carry one spur. The Court of Claims decided that for the 1953 ceremony Lord Hastings and Lord Churston should do duty, it being referred to Her Majesty to determine how their service should be performed.

STAFF OF ST. EDWARD. Carried by a peer walking immediately before the Queen in the Coronation procession in Westminster Abbey. It is an object of sceptre-like appearance, made of gold, with a steel foot, and is surmounted by a golden mound and cross. The original Staff, destroyed by the Puritans, contained what was claimed to be a relic of the Cross. Formerly it was placed in the Sovereign's hands on entering the Abbey.

STONE OF SCONE. Is incorporated in the Coronation Chair in which the Sovereigns of England have received the Crown ever since the time of King Edward II, nearly six hundred and fifty years ago. The Stone had previously been the seat on which the Kings of Scotland had been crowned, and it was captured by Edward I, Hammer of the Scots, during his final campaign in Scotland. The Stone was named after the town of Scone, near Perth, which had been the place of Scottish coronations since the year 1153. When Edward I proclaimed himself King of the Northern Kingdom, he decided to raze the Abbey of Scone to the ground, and he dispatched to London a number of relics which the Scots prized, including the Stone. Edward died during the campaign, and his son, Edward II, was the first English Sovereign to receive the crown seated above the Stone.

Staff of St. Edward

The Scots made every effort to recover the relic. In the reign of Edward III a treaty was entered into to bring to a close the long wars between the two kingdoms, one of the conditions of which was that Scotland's lost relics should be returned. All were sent back, the Stone alone excepted. When James I of England was crowned in Westminster Abbey in 1603 a Scottish king was seated once again on the Stone of Scone after a lapse of 300 years. There was seen fulfilled the ancient prophecy:

> Unless the fixed decrees of Fate give way,
> The Scots shall govern and the sceptre sway
> Where'er this stone they find
> And its dread sound obey.

The belief expressed in this doggerel is only one, and by no means the most ancient, of the legends which have clustered round the Stone of Scone. According to the legends it was on the Stone of Scone that Jacob rested his head at Bethel when he saw the vision of the angels ascending and descending from heaven. By the descendants of the Patriarch it was conveyed to Egypt. Next it was taken to Spain by Gathelus, son of Cecrops, builder of Athens, who had married an Egyptian wife. At Brigantia, Gathelus sat on the Stone when he gave laws and administered justice to his people.

Next to Ireland the Stone was transported by Simon

Stone of Scone

Brech 700 years before the Christian era. It was set up upon the Hill of Tara and upon it the Irish kings were initiated. Lia-Fail, the Stone of Destiny, was now a testing-stone. If the king placed upon it was the true successor of his predecessor the Stone indicated its confirmation by remaining silent. But if the succession were false it groaned aloud with thunder.

At last the Stone reached Scotland, borne there by Fergus, founder of the Scottish monarchy. For safe keeping he placed it in the vaults of the royal castle of Dunstaffnage, where a hole in the castle wall is still pointed to as being the spot it occupied. Finally, in the year 840, Kenneth II transferred it to the Monastery of Scone, because the last battle of the Picts was fought there. As in the Abbey today, it was contained in the seat of a royal chair, and under the care of the monks it remained at Scone until the time of Edward I.

Dean Stanley, Historian of Westminster Abbey, seventy years ago invited Professor Ramsay, then the leading geologist in England, to examine the Stone. A few grains were detached from it, sufficient for a microscopic examination to be made and chemical tests to be carried out. Professor Ramsay reported the following facts:

> The Coronation Stone consists of a dull reddish or purple sandstone with a few small embedded pebbles.
>
> The country around Scone is formed of old red sandstone, and the tints of different portions of that formation are so various that it is quite possible the Stone may have been derived from one of its strata.
>
> There can be little doubt that Dunstaffnage Castle was built from rocks of the surrounding neighbourhood, the sandstone strata of which are described as dull reddish or purplish. This precisely agrees with the character of the Coronation Stone itself.
>
> It is extremely improbable that the Stone has been derived from any of the rocks of the Hill of Tara. They do not present the texture or red colour characteristic of the Coronation Stone.
>
> Neither can it have been taken from the rocks of Iona. There is no red sandstone on this island.
>
> That it belonged originally to the rocks round Bethel is equally unlikely, since according to reports they are formed of strata of limestone.
>
> The rocks of Egypt consist chiefly of limestone, and I have never heard of any strata occurring there similar to the red sandstone.
>
> To my eye (he concludes), the Stone appears as if it had originally been prepared for building purposes but had never been used.

At Christmas, 1950, the nation was astounded by the news that the Stone had been stolen from the Abbey in the early hours of Christmas Day. In the long inquiries that followed it became known that it had been taken by three Scottish nationalist students. Not before April 11 was the Stone recovered by the police. It had been deposited at the high altar of the ruined Abbey of Arbroath, in Scotland, and was returned to Westminster Abbey on April 13, 1951, 109 days after its disappearance. Thereafter it was kept hidden in the Islip vault until it was restored to public view in its traditional place in the Coronation Chair on February 26, 1952, twenty days after the accession of Queen Elizabeth and 429 days after it had been stolen.

SUCCESSION TO THE THRONE.

The line of succession to the Throne is:

1. The Duke of Cornwall.
2. Princess Anne.
3. Princess Margaret.
4. The Duke of Gloucester.
5. Prince William of Gloucester.
6. Prince Richard of Gloucester.
7. The Duke of Kent.
8. Prince Michael of Kent.
9. Princess Alexandra of Kent.
10. The Princess Royal.
11. The Earl of Harewood.

Inheritance of the Crown follows the rules for the succession to landed estates under feudal law. The Crown descends lineally to the issue of the reigning monarch, with preference of male over female heirs; the right of primogeniture is strictly adhered to. Thus on the death of King Henry VIII the young Prince Edward succeeded before his elder sister, and then on his death the elder sister Mary reigned before Elizabeth, her younger stepsister. The lineal descendants of any deceased heir stand in the same position as their ancestor, if living, would have done. Thus the children of the late Duke of Kent have a prior place to their aunt, the Princess Royal. The succession has been determined from time to time by Acts of Parliament, on the last occasion by the statute providing for the abdication of King Edward VIII and the succession of his brother as George VI. The governing Statute now in force is the Act of Settlement passed in 1701 in the reign of William III designed to ensure that none but a Protestant should occupy the English throne. This transferred the succession to Princess Sophia, grand-daughter of King James I, "the nearest person of the ancient blood royal not incapacitated by professing the Popish religion".

SUPERTUNICA, or CLOSE PALL. A kind of tunic in which the Queen is attired during the Coronation. (*See* Vestments.)

SWORDS. There are five swords in the Regalia, all of which are used in the Coronation service.

The Sword of State is thirty-two inches long and two inches wide, has a gold hilt and quillion (crosspiece between

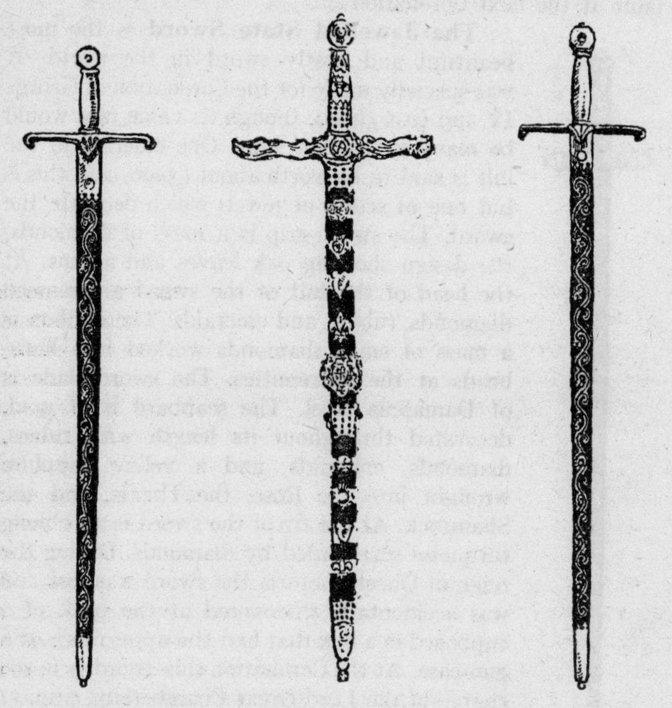

Sword Spiritual Sword of State Sword Temporal

hilt and blade), and rests in a scabbard of crimson velvet. The quillion has the representation of a lion on one side and a unicorn on the other. A harp, fleur-de-lis, and a portcullis are represented on the blade hilt; a thistle, an orb, and other emblems are represented on the pommel. It is carried by a peer in procession at the Coronation and on State occasions, with the point upwards. During the service, because of its weight, its place is taken by the lighter Jewelled State Sword.

The Sword of State was by some means forgotten at the Coronation of George III. When the King complained to the Deputy Earl Marshal, he acknowledged the omission, but promised that care should be taken to avoid a similar fault at the next Coronation!

Jewelled State Sword

The Jewelled State Sword is the most beautiful and costly sword in the world. It was specially made for the Coronation of George IV and cost £6000, though its value now would be many times that sum. One emerald in the hilt is said to be worth about £3000, and this is but one of scores of jewels which decorate the sword. The sword-grip is a mass of diamonds, the design showing oak leaves and acorns. At the head of the hilt of the sword are massed diamonds, rubies, and emeralds. The quillion is a mass of small diamonds worked into lions' heads at the extremities. The sword-blade is of Damascus steel. The scabbard is of gold, decorated throughout its length with rubies, diamonds, emeralds, and a yellow sapphire wrought into the Rose, the Thistle, and the Shamrock. At the tip of the sword is an oblong turquoise surrounded by diamonds. During the reign of Queen Victoria the sword was lost and was accidentally discovered at the back of a cupboard in a box that had the appearance of a gun-case. At the Coronation this sword is in the charge of the Lord Great Chamberlain, who, at the appointed time in the service, hands it over in exchange to the peer who bears the Sword of State. It is delivered to the Archbishop, who at the end of a prayer hands it to the Queen. After the Archbishop's exhortation the Queen approaches the Altar and there presents it in its scabbard. The sword is redeemed by the payment of 100 shillings and returned to the peer who carried it.

The Sword Spiritual is a copy of one of three similar swords sent by Pope Clement to King Henry VIII when he conferred upon him the title of Defender of the Faith. It has an obtuse point, an indication that in the ecclesiastical courts the sentences have not the sharpness of death. At the Corona-

Knight of the Thistle

tion it is carried before the Queen sheathed, and with point upward. Field Marshal Lord Milne was the bearer of this sword at the Coronation of George VI.

The Sword of Mercy (*see* CURTANA.)

The Sword Temporal has a sharp point, but is otherwise

similar to the Sword Spiritual, and is carried in a similar manner at the Coronation. It was carried by Marshal of the Royal Air Force Lord Trenchard at the last Coronation.

T

THISTLE, ORDER OF THE. This Scottish Order of Knighthood is reputed to be of remote origin and to be associated with James V. It is known, however, that James II of the United Kingdoms established or revived it in 1687 and assigned to it the royal chapel at Holyrood. The Order collapsed through the Revolution of the following year but was re-established by Queen Anne in 1703, with its chapel in St. Giles's Cathedral, Edinburgh.

TRUMPETS. Originally there were sixteen silver trumpets, but at some time one was lost and has not been recovered or replaced. The trumpets are of the ordinary cavalry kind. From each hangs a banneret of crimson silk embroidered with gold displaying the cipher of the monarch and the Royal Arms. At the Coronation, after the presentation of the Queen to her people by the Archbishop of Canterbury, and after they have signified their acceptance of her, a fanfare is sounded on the fifteen trumpets. The trumpets are also used when the Heralds make proclamations in the Queen's name, e.g. the Accession, the Proclaiming of Peace, etc.

U

USHER OF THE WHITE ROD OF SCOTLAND. (*See* Walker Trustees.)

V

VESTMENTS. During the Coronation service the Queen is attired in a number of vestments similar to those of a priest or bishop. They emphasize the priest-like nature of the office. Upon her head is placed a square of linen called the Amice or Coif .Next she puts on the Colobium Sindonis, a kind of surplice

Imperial Mantle

without sleeves, made of fine white cambric. Over this is placed the Supertunica, or close pall of cloth-of-gold, a long tunic richly worked in gold thread. The Armill, a narrow strip of silk shaped like a stole, is passed over the shoulders.

Finally, the Imperial Mantle is placed on Her Majesty. The

Mantle is otherwise called the Pallium or Dalmatic robe. It is similar to the cope of an ecclesiastical dignitary, and is richly embroidered in designs incorporating the national emblems of rose, shamrock, and thistle.

VIRGE. Alternative name for the Rod of Equity. (See Sceptre.) A sceptre topped with a dove which is placed in the Queen's left hand.

W

WALES, PRINCE OF. The traditional title of Prince of Wales is not an automatic birthright but is by individual investment at the Sovereign's pleasure. When the Heir Apparent is made Prince of Wales he is at the same time created Earl of Chester. Caernarvon Town Council decided on March 4, 1952, to petition the Queen to proclaim the Duke of Cornwall Prince of Wales at Caernarvon Castle.

The first English Prince of Wales was Edward I's second son, who became Edward II. He was born at Caernarvon Castle in 1284 and created Prince of Wales in 1301. There have been twenty-one holders of the title. Edward VII was given it a day before he was a month old in 1841. Ten months after his own accession he made his son, George V, Prince of Wales at the age of thirty-six. The last holder of the title, now Duke of Windsor, was created at the age of sixteen on June 23, 1910, a month and a half after his father became King. He was invested at Caernarvon Castle on July 13 the following year, a month after the Coronation. In the following list the date of creation as Prince of Wales precedes the name.

1301—Edward of Caernarvon; born 1284, son of Edward I; reigned as Edward II, 1307–1327.

1343—Edward the Black Prince; born 1330, son of Edward III; died 1376.

1377—Richard of Bordeaux; born 1367, son of the Black Prince; reigned as Richard II, 1377–1399.

1399—Henry of Monmouth; born 1387, son of Henry IV; reigned as Henry V, 1413–1422.

1454—Edward of Lancaster; born 1453, son of Henry VI; killed in battle, 1471.
1471—Edward of York; born 1470, son of Edward IV; reigned as Edward V, 1483.
1483—Edward Earl of Salisbury; born 1474, son of Richard III; died 1484.
1489—Arthur Tudor; born 1486, son of Henry VII; died 1502.
1503—Henry Tudor; born 1491, son of Henry VII; reigned as Henry VIII, 1509–1547.
1510—Infant son of King Henry VIII hastily created before his death at age of two months.
1610—Henry Stuart; born 1594, son of James I; died 1612.
1616—Charles Stuart; born 1600, son of James I; reigned as Charles I, 1626–1649.
1630—Charles Stuart; born 1630, son of Charles I; reigned as Charles II, 1661–1685.
1688—James Francis Edward Stuart; born 1688, son of James II; died 1766.
1714—George Augustus of Hanover; born 1683, son of George I; reigned as George II, 1727–1760.
1729—Frederick Louis of Hanover; born 1707, son of George II; died 1751.
1751—George William Frederick; born 1738, son of preceding prince; reigned as George III, 1760–1820.
1762—George Augustus Frederick; born 1762, son of George III; reigned as George IV, 1820–1830.
1841—Albert Edward; born 1841, son of Queen Victoria; reigned as Edward VII, 1901–1910.
1901—George Frederick Ernest Albert; born 1865, son of Edward VII; reigned as George V, 1910–1936.
1910—Edward Albert Christian George Andrew Patrick David; born 1894, son of George V; reigned as Edward VIII, 1936.

WALKER TRUSTEES. The Walker Trustees claim to exercise the office of Usher of the White Rod of Scotland by deputy; the petitioners were incorporated in 1877 by Act of

Parliament ("The Walker Trust Act"). Their claim was that the office was conveyed to them by the trust-deed of their foundress, the late Miss Mary Walker of Coates and Drumsheugh, in the County of Midlothian, "who had inherited the office as eventual heiress of her sister, Miss Barbara Walker, and their brother, Sir Patrick Walker". That is to say, Sir Patrick Walker, who attended George IV's coronation as Usher of the White Rod, bequeathed the office to his sisters. The Usher of the White Rod was not permitted to be present at the coronations of King William IV and Queen Victoria, but at the coronations of King Edward VII, King George V, and King George VI the claimants' right to be present by deputy was approved. The claim has again been allowed for the 1953 ceremony.

WESTMINSTER ABBEY has been the scene of the crowning of the English Sovereigns for little short of nine hundred years. The building which we call the Abbey was formerly the church of the Benedictine monastery dedicated to St. Peter. The first church is supposed to have been erected on the site over one thousand seven hundred years ago, when England was a Roman province. Then the Christians were ejected and the place became a temple of the god Apollo. King Lucius, one of the earliest of Christian kings in England, is credited with the re-establishment of Christian worship. According to tradition, the establishment of an Abbey at Westminster was brought about in the year 616 by a Saxon called Sebert, who is variously described as a King of Essex and a private citizen of London. The isle of Thorne, on which the foundations were laid, was then a "jungle" of a place with an evil reputation. It was convenient for monks in that there were good springs of water and good fishing in the Thames. There is a legend which narrates how St. Peter himself performed the dedication ceremony of this new Abbey, anticipating in this Mellitus, Bishop of London.

Four hundred years later a new and greater Abbey was built at Westminster by Edward the Confessor. Again there are legends of the intervention of St. Peter in securing the patronage of the Saxon king for Westminster Monastery.

Edward as a young man had to leave England because of the Danes and seek refuge on the Continent. As a refugee he prayed to St. Peter, whom he held in special veneration, to secure his return to his native England; he swore an oath that if his wish were granted he would make a pilgrimage to St. Peter's grave in Rome. It came about that his wish was granted and he

Westminster Abbey

returned to England to be crowned king. But when he announced his intention of carrying out his pledge and making a pilgrimage to Rome, his counsellors objected. They pointed out that during the King's long absence the country would be likely to suffer many perils. So Edward was prevailed upon to send a deputation to Rome to seek release from his pledge, which was granted him on condition that he founded or restored a monastery dedicated to St. Peter. For some time he was in a state of perplexity as to where his patronage should be bestowed, for many Abbeys of St. Peter had claims on the royal favour. Ultimately the decision was made in favour of the foundation of St. Peter of Westminster on the strength of a monk's dream. This man, Wulsine, one of the Westminster brethren, related that St. Peter appeared to him and spoke of the Abbey in the west part of London, which, for the sins of the people, from rich had become poor, and from honourable had been made despicable. "This," commanded the Saint, "let the King by my command restore and make a dwelling of monks, stately build and amply endow; it shall be no less than the house of God and the gates of Heaven." Accepting this guidance, King Edward set about the task of creating a new Abbey at Westminster, with a right royal lavishness in the discharge of his pledge.

He lavished upon it one tenth of the property of the kingdom. To superintend the work the better he built a palace for himself beside the Thames—the Palace of Westminster. For fifteen years he directed the erection of his wonder church. He sent a deputation to Rome to obtain special privileges for the new Abbey. He bestowed on it a set of relics which were the envy of every other religious house in the country.

Fifteen years' work of building was at last completed. King Edward's new church was one of the sights of London. There was nothing like it in the land. As the year 1065 drew to its close, the day of consecration approached when the royal builder would put the final seal of completion to his work. Edward looked forward to the day as one of the crowning moments in his life; but as the final arrangements were made, his strength, overtaxed by his labours, began to leave him. On Christmas night the King collapsed. It was a warning that he could not mistake. He ordered that the solemnities of the consecration should be hurried forward.

Fearful lest delay should prevent him from taking part in the one act on which his entire hopes were now fixed, he directed that December 28 should be the date of the consecration, even though it was the unluckiest day of the year, the

Feast of the Holy Innocents, the day on which no great task was by choice begun, because of the ill luck with which it was associated.

It was too late. Death was already upon the King. The consecration was carried out, but Edward could not be present. His place was taken by his Queen, Edith. On the evening of Childermas the King sank into a stupor. He lingered for a few days, but only just survived the new year. His burial was the first ceremonial in his newly completed Abbey.

On Christmas Day 1066 William the Conqueror was crowned in Westminster Abbey. His was the first coronation that we can say with certainty took place there, for it is in dispute whether Harold received the crown at Westminster or St. Paul's. It was William's claim that he succeeded to the crown by right. His aim was to make it appear in the eyes of his subjects that he was following as lawful successor to the Saxon Edward. There could be no more eloquent demonstration than for him to be crowned in the church the Confessor had built, on the very spot where the remains of the Confessor lay. Thus was begun the long series of coronations which, with unbroken link, connect the reigns of the last king of Anglo-Saxon England and the first crowning of a sovereign of the House of Windsor. Two kings alone are an exception in the line—the boy Edward V, who was murdered, and Edward VIII, who abdicated. One was crowned, but never lived to reign—the son of Henry III, whose coronation was carried out during his father's lifetime, but whose death took place before his father's, so that he did not survive to wear as king the crown that he received as prince.

During the nine centuries which have now nearly run their course since the Confessor's day, there has been much rebuilding of the Abbey, so that little of his work now remains. Henry III was the great rebuilder. He decided that the remains of so holy a saint as the Confessor must be housed in the most magnificent edifice that could be constructed. In the year 1245 he gave orders for reconstruction on the model of the French churches then building at Amiens and Rheims. Like the

Dean of Westminster

Confessor, Henry lavished vast sums of money upon his royal Abbey. He even pawned the royal jewels in order to raise money.

Twenty-four years were occupied by Henry's builders in erecting the eastern end of the church, the transepts, and five bays of the nave as they stand today. In the year 1269 the King, assisted by his sons, and in the presence of the peers of the realm, bore the coffin of the Confessor to its new magnificent shrine, to the east of the High Altar.

The Plantagenets' church is the essential base of the Abbey that we know. The Chapel to the east was constructed by Henry VII; the twin towers at the western entrance were added by Sir Christopher Wren; Sir Gilbert Scott was responsible for the front of the north side opposite St. Margaret's Church, perhaps the best-known aspect of the Abbey.

WESTMINSTER, DEAN OF. The Dean and Chapter of Westminster have the right to be present at the Coronation ceremony to instruct the Queen in the rites and ceremonies;

Windsor Castle

and to assist the Archbishop of Canterbury; and to have cloth, etc., for fee. They do this as inheritors of the rights and privileges possessed by the Abbot and brethren of St. Peter. The present Dean of Westminster, Dr. Alan Campbell Don, a Scot, has occupied the office since 1946. He was born on January 3, 1885. Formerly Sub-Dean and Canon, and Rector of St. Margaret's, Westminster. K.C.V.O., 1948. Educated at Rugby and Magdalen, Oxford, he began in his father's Dundee jute business. Provost of St. Paul's Cathedral Church, Dundee, 1921–31; then for ten years chaplain to Archbishop Lord Lang, his godfather. After the theft of the Coronation Stone on Christmas Day, 1950, he broadcast an appeal for help in its recovery.

WESTMINSTER SCHOOLBOYS lead the shout of acclamation in Westminster Abbey after the new sovereign has been presented to the assembly by the Archbishop of Canterbury.

WINDSOR CASTLE. For more than eight centuries a residence of the Sovereigns of England, this is one of the finest castles in Europe. It owes its origin to William the Conqueror's appreciation of its commanding position on a cliff above the Thames and its grandeur to Edward III, who was born there. Edward made great additions, entailed by his institution of the Order of the Garter in 1348. Many English Kings and Queens rest there and all since George III have been buried at Windsor. Queen Victoria was laid to rest beside the Prince Consort in the magnificent mausoleum at Frogmore.

WINDSOR, DUKE OF. The title conferred after his abdication upon King Edward VIII. First son of the Duke and Duchess of York, who reigned as King George V and Queen Mary, he was born on June 23, 1894, at White Lodge, Richmond Park. He was christened Edward Albert Christian George Andrew Patrick David. At the age of thirteen he was entered as a naval cadet at Osborne, and went on to the Royal Naval College at Dartmouth. After the accession to the throne of his father, King George V, he was created Prince of Wales, and his investiture took place on July 13, 1911, at Caernarvon Castle. The Prince of Wales became an undergraduate at Magdalen College, Oxford, in the following year. His studies were cut short by the war. On August 8, 1914, he was gazetted Second Lieutenant in the First Battalion Grenadier Guards, and two days later joined the battalion. In November 1914 he was appointed aide-de-camp to General Sir John French, Commander-in-Chief of the British Expeditionary Force, and crossed to France to proceed to French's headquarters at St. Omer. In the second year of the war he was promoted to captain, and was attached to the Mediterranean Expeditionary Force. Later he visited the Italian Military Headquarters. In those four years of war he mixed with men, and, as he said in a public speech later, found his manhood. After the war the Prince of Wales set up a separate establishment for himself at York House. His series of Empire tours began in August 1919, when in H.M.S. *Renown* he sailed for Canada. In the following year he visited New Zealand and Australia. In 1921 he visited the United States at the invitation of President Coolidge, with whom he lunched at White House. In 1925 he journeyed to South and West Africa. After a visit to Canada early in 1927 he set out in September of that year for a big-game trip to East Africa, which was brought to a sudden close by his father's illness, which caused him to hurry home, covering 6500 miles in ten days. He succeeded to the throne, on the death of King George V, on January 21, 1936. His reign lasted for 325 days, and since the Norman Conquest there has been only one shorter—that of the child Edward V, who, with his brother, was murdered in the Tower of London.

The abdication of King Edward VIII resulted from the fact that he wished to marry Mrs. Ernest Simpson. This lady was born in the United States of America in 1896. She was the daughter of Teackle Wallis Warfield and his wife Alys Montague, of Baltimore, Ohio. She was christened Bessie Wallis. In 1918 she married Lieutenant Earl Winfield Spencer, a United States naval airman, at Christ's Protestant Episcopal Church, Baltimore.

She first saw the Duke of Windsor, then Prince of Wales, at a naval ball held in the United States in 1920. In 1926 she was presented at Court at Buckingham Palace. In 1927 she obtained a divorce from Mr. Spencer, and in 1928 she was married at Chelsea to Mr. Ernest Aldrich Simpson, whose former marriage had been dissolved.

In 1936 the names of Mr. and Mrs. Ernest Simpson appeared in the *Court Circular* with those of other guests at the King's Derby Day dinner-party at St. James's Palace. In July Mrs. Simpson's name appeared in the *Court Circular* as one of the guests at the King's dinner-party at York House, which was attended by the Duke and Duchess of York. Mrs. Simpson was a member of the party which accompanied King Edward on his holiday cruise to the Adriatic in the yacht *Nahlin*, and in September she was one of his guests at Balmoral. On October 27, at the Suffolk Assizes at Ipswich, Mr. Justice Hawke granted Mrs. Simpson a decree nisi of divorce against her husband. King Edward decided to abdicate rather than give up his intention to marry Mrs. Simpson. As Duke of Windsor he was married to her on June 3, 1937.

WINDSOR, HOUSE OF. The name now borne by the Sovereigns of England. King George V decided during the First World War to discontinue the style of the House of Hanover by which our kings had been known since this line was begun with King George I in 1715. The change was made by a proclamation dated July 17, 1917, which stated:

> Whereas We, having taken into consideration the Name and Title of Our Royal House and family, have determined that henceforth Our House and Family shall be styled and known as the House and Family of Windsor. . . .
>
> We, out of Our Royal Will and Authority, do hereby declare and announce that as from the date of this Our Royal Proclamation Our House and Family shall be styled and known as the House and Family of Windsor, and that all the descendants in the male line of Our said Grandmother Queen Victoria who are subjects of these Realms, other than female descendants who may marry or may have married, shall bear the said Name of Windsor.
>
> And do hereby further declare and announce that We for Ourselves and for and on behalf of Our descendants and all the other descendants of Our said Grandmother Queen Victoria who are subjects of these Realms, relinquish and enjoin the discontinuance of the use of the Degrees, Styles, Dignities, Titles, and Honours of Dukes and Duchesses of Saxony and Princes and Princesses of Saxe-Coburg and Gotha, and all other German Degrees, Styles, Dignities, Titles, Honours, and Appellations to Us or to them heretofore belonging or appertaining.

King George V was the last Sovereign of the House of Hanover and the first of the House of Windsor. King George VI was the first Sovereign of the House of Windsor to be crowned as such. It is clear from the phrasing of George V's proclamation, particularly his significant use of the word "henceforth", that it was his wish and intention that the Reigning House should continue to be known as the House of Windsor, irrespective of whether the Sovereign was a King or a Queen Regnant. The Duke of Edinburgh, on becoming a British subject before his marriage, had adopted his uncle's surname of Mountbatten. The question, now that the succession had passed to the female line, was settled by the Queen in the following announcement, dated April 9, 1952, from Clarence House:

> "The Queen to-day declared in Council her will and pleasure that she and her children shall be styled and known as the House and Family of Windsor, and that her descendants, other than female descendants who marry, and their descendants, shall bear the name of Windsor."

Y

YEOMEN OF THE GUARD. This ancient royal bodyguard, a corps whose expenses are borne by the Sovereign's Civil List, was founded by Henry VII in 1485, and made its first appearance at the Coronation of that Sovereign. The members of this, the oldest military company in the world, still wear fifteenth-century costume.

In State processions the Yeomen of the Guard, with the Gentlemen-at-Arms, appear in the monarch's retinue. In the Coronation procession to Westminster Abbey a Yeoman of the Guard walks at each wheel of the State Coach and two Yeomen at each door, while the Captain of the Yeomen of the Guard rides on one side of the coach. In the Abbey the officers of the company are usually stationed near the choir door, and the privates in the nave on the outside of the entrance to the choir. The officers are eight in number: a Captain, who is always a Peer; a Lieutenant; a Clerk of the Cheque, the Adjutant and Secretary of the Corps, but not, as the title might suggest, the Paymaster; an Ensign; and four Exons (or "exempts", an "exempt" having been an officer in an ancient French corps of a like nature). The officers of the company are: Captain, Earl of Onslow, M.C., T.D.; Lieutenant, Maj.-Gen. Sir Allan Adair, Bt., C.B., D.S.O., M.C.; Clerk of the Cheque and Adjutant, Lt.-Col. R. C. Bingham, D.S.O.; Ensign, Lt.-Col. V. B. Turner, V.C.; Exons, Brig. W. G. Carr, D.S.O., Lt.-Col. G. H. Grosvenor.

Yeoman of the Guard

Some of the non-commissioned officers of the Yeomen of the Guard bear quaint titles—for example, Yeomen Bed-goers and Yeomen Bed-hangers. The men number one hundred, and are old soldiers. The Yeomen are popularly known as "Beefeaters", as are also, in error, the Warders of the Tower of London. This

Archbishop of York

mistake arises from the similarities in their uniforms, but the fact is that the Yeomen of the Guard and the Warders of the Tower are separate bodies.

YORK, ARCHBISHOP OF. Assists the Archbishop of Canterbury in the Coronation service. The See of York is the most ancient bishopric, having been founded soon after Christianity was established in Britain in the year A.D. 180. It was, however, overthrown, and the present line of succession dates from its restoration in the year 632 by Gregory. The

Archbishop of York is entitled to be styled His Grace. He is Primate of England by Divine Permission, not as is the Archbishop of Canterbury—Primate of All England by Divine Providence. In precedence he ranks third amongst the peers not of Royal Family, the Lord Chancellor taking second place between the Primates of Canterbury and York. The present, the ninety-first holder of the office, is the Most Rev. and Rt. Hon. Cyril Forster Garbett, Archbishop since 1942. He was born on February 6, 1875. Son of a former chaplain of the East India Company, he was educated at Portsmouth and at Keble and Cuddesdon Colleges, Oxford, and was elected President of the Oxford Union. As assistant curate on the staff at Portsea of Cosmo Lang, he attracted the attention of the future Archbishop of Canterbury. He became Bishop of Southwark in 1919 and Bishop of Winchester in 1932. He made a moving address at the wedding of the Queen and the Duke of Edinburgh in Westminster Abbey in 1947 and read the final prayers at the funeral of George VI at St. George's Chapel, Windsor.

Z

ZADOK, THE PRIEST, is mentioned at the Coronation service during the ceremony of anointing the Queen with oil. Zadok was a priest of the Jews who took part in the ceremony of making Solomon king, as is described in the Bible: "And Zadok, the priest, took an horn of oil out of the tabernacle and anointed Solomon. And they blew the trumpet; and all the people said, God save King Solomon." (1 Kings, i, 39.) The words, to music by Handel, are sung as an anthem at the Coronation service.

APPENDIX

KINGS AND QUEENS AND CORONATIONS

WILLIAM I Born Falaise, Normandy, 1027; crowned Monday, Dec. 25, 1066; died France 1087

WILLIAM II Born probably Rouen, 1060; crowned Sunday, Sept. 26, 1087; died New Forest 1100

HENRY I Born Yorkshire 1068; crowned Sunday, Aug. 5, 1100; died France 1135

STEPHEN Born Chartres 1101; crowned Thursday, Dec. 26, 1135; died Dover 1154

HENRY II Born Le Mans 1133; crowned Sunday, Dec. 19, 1154; died France 1189

RICHARD I Born Oxford 1157; crowned Sunday, Sept. 3, 1189; died Chalers 1199

JOHN Born Woodstock 1167; crowned Thursday, May 27, 1199; died Newark 1216

HENRY III Born Winchester 1206; crowned Friday, Oct. 28, 1216; died Westminster 1272

EDWARD I Born Westminster Palace 1239; crowned Sunday, Aug. 19, 1275; died Burgh-on-Sands, near Carlisle, 1307

EDWARD II Born Carnarvon 1284; crowned Sunday, Feb. 25, 1307; deposed and murdered Berkeley Castle 1327

EDWARD III Born Windsor 1312; crowned Sunday or Monday, Feb. 1 or 2, 1327; died Sheen 1377

RICHARD II Born Bordeaux 1367; crowned Thursday, July 16, 1377; dethroned and murdered Pomfret Castle 1399

HENRY IV Born Lincolnshire 1367; crowned Tuesday, Oct. 13, 1399; died Westminster, after fit in Jerusalem Chamber, 1413

HENRY V Born Monmouth 1387; crowned Sunday, April 9, 1413; died France 1422

HENRY VI Born Windsor 1421; crowned Sunday, Nov. 6, 1429; dethroned 1461; murdered in the Tower 1471

EDWARD IV Born Rouen 1442; crowned Monday, June 29, 1461; died Westminster 1483

EDWARD V Born Westminster 1470; never crowned; deposed 1483; murdered in the Tower with his brother Richard by Duke of Gloucester

RICHARD III Born Fotheringay Castle 1452; crowned Sunday, July 6, 1483; slain at Battle of Bosworth 1485

HENRY VII Born Pembroke Castle 1457; crowned Sunday, Oct. 30, 1485; died Richmond 1509

HENRY VIII Born Greenwich Palace 1491; crowned Sunday, June 24, 1509; died Westminster 1547

EDWARD VI Born Hampton Court 1537; crowned Sunday, Feb. 20, 1547; died Greenwich Palace 1553

MARY Born Greenwich Palace 1516; crowned Sunday, Oct. 1, 1553; died St. James's Palace 1558

ELIZABETH I Born Greenwich Palace 1533; crowned Sunday, Jan. 15, 1559; died Richmond 1603

JAMES I Born Edinburgh Castle 1566; crowned Monday, July 25, 1603; died Theobalds, Hertfordshire, 1625

CHARLES I Born Dunfermlime Castle 1600; crowned Thursday, Feb. 2, 1626; executed Whitehall 1649

CHARLES II Born St. James's Palace 1630; crowned Tuesday, April 23, 1661; died Whitehall 1685

JAMES II Born St. James's Palace 1633; crowned Thursday, April 23, 1686; abdicated 1689; died in exile 1701

WILLIAM III AND MARY William born The Hague 1650; crowned Thursday, April 11, 1689; died Kensington 1702; Mary born St. James's Palace 1662; crowned April 1689; died Kensington Palace 1694

ANNE Born St. James's Palace 1665; crowned Thursday, April 23, 1702; died St. James's 1714

GEORGE I Born Hanover 1660; crowned Wednesday, Oct. 20, 1714; died Hanover 1727

GEORGE II Born Hanover 1683; crowned Wednesday, Oct. 11, 1727; died Kensington 1760

GEORGE III Born St. James's 1738; crowned Tuesday, Sept. 22, 1761; died Windsor 1820

GEORGE IV Born St. James's 1762; crowned Thursday, July 19, 1821; died Windsor 1830

WILLIAM IV Born Buckingham Palace 1765; crowned Thursday, Sept. 8, 1831; died Windsor 1837

VICTORIA Born Kensington Palace 1819; crowned Thursday, June 28, 1838; died Osborne 1901

EDWARD VII Born Buckingham Palace 1841; crowned Saturday, Aug. 9, 1902; died Buckingham Palace 1910

GEORGE V Born Marlborough House 1865; crowned Thursday, June 22, 1911; died Sandringham 1936

EDWARD VIII Born White Lodge, Sheen 1894; abdicated Dec. 11, 1936

GEORGE VI Born Sandringham, Dec. 14, 1895; married 1923 Lady Elizabeth Bowes-Lyon, daughter of Earl of Strathmore; crowned Wednesday, May 12, 1937; died Sandringham, Feb. 6, 1952

ELIZABETH II Born 17, Bruton Street, London, April 21, 1926; married Nov. 20, 1947. Philip, Duke of Edinburgh.

LONG MAY SHE REIGN!

The actual moment of Coronation

QUEEN ELIZABETH'S TITLE

A CHANGE in the title of the Sovereign designed to bring it into accord with the current constitutional relations within the Commonwealth, was announced on December 12. It was decided upon by Ministers representing the various countries of the Commonwealth meeting in London for the Economic Conference. As a result, Queen Elizabeth's title for use in the United Kingdom is:

> ELIZABETH THE SECOND, BY THE GRACE OF GOD OF THE UNITED KINGDOM OF GREAT BRITAIN AND NORTHERN IRELAND AND OF HER OTHER REALMS AND TERRITORIES QUEEN, HEAD OF THE COMMONWEALTH, DEFENDER OF THE FAITH

Her Majesty will also be Queen of Canada, of Australia, of New Zealand and of South Africa, titles not borne by her predecessors. The Royal style will be:

CANADA.—Elizabeth the Second, by the Grace of God of the United Kingdom, Canada and her other Realms and Territories Queen, Head of the Commonwealth, Defender of the Faith.

AUSTRALIA.—Elizabeth the Second, by the Grace of God of the United Kingdom, Australia and her other Realms and Territories Queen, Head of the Commonwealth, Defender of the Faith.

NEW ZEALAND.—Elizabeth the Second, by the Grace of God of the United Kingdom, New Zealand and her other Realms and Territories Queen, Head of the Commonwealth, Defender of the Faith.

South Africa.—Elizabeth the Second, Queen of South Africa and of her other Realms and Territories, Head of the Commonwealth.

Pakistan.—Elizabeth the Second, Queen of the United Kingdom and of her other Realms and Territories, Head of the Commonwealth.

Ceylon.—Elizabeth the Second, Queen of Ceylon and of her other Realms and Territories, Head of the Commonwealth.

MAP OF CORONATION PROCESSION ROUTE

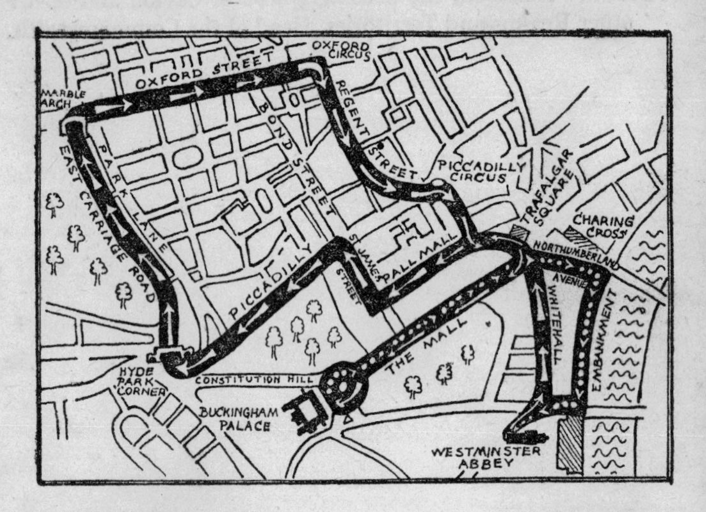